AF565003

POLITICAL MYSTERIES

POLITICAL MYSTERIES

K.R. Malkani

Ocean Books Pvt. Ltd.
ISO 9001:2015 Publishers

Published by
Ocean Books (P) Ltd.
4/19 Asaf Ali Road,
New Delhi-110 002 (INDIA)
e-mail-info@oceanbooks.in

ISBN 978-81-8430-629-3
POLITICAL MYSTERIES
by Shri K.R. Malkani

Edition
2026

Price
₹ 350.00 (Rupees Three Hundred Fifty only)

Printed at
Narula Printers, Delhi

Contents

Introduction

Some ten years ago, a good friend of mine, Shri R. Chandrachudan, said to me that Gandhiji had been got bumped off by the British. I have known him since 1948 when he was a senior special correspondent of *The Hindustan Times* and me a sub-editor preparing the obituaries of ageing leaders like Mr. Jinnah, Maulana Azad, Sardar Patel, Acharya Kripalani, Sarojini Naidu, Sri Aurobindo and others.

We had all known that Nathuram Godse and his friends had killed Gandhiji. How did the British come into that picture? I could not believe my ears. But Chandrachudan was a senior, serious and seasoned journalist. And he used to be the right-hand man of Devadas Gandhi, Managing Editor of *The Hindustan Times* and son of the Mahatma himself. And he was saying it. So his statement could not be lightly dismissed.

And then something happened. The BBC announced on Saturday, July 19, 1997, that Aung San, the top Burmese nationalist leader, had been liquidated by the British on July 19, 1947 (vide *The Asian Age*, July 22, 1997).

And that rang a bell. If the British could admittedly murder Aung San, they were even more likely to see much bigger challengers like Netaji Subhas Chandra Bose and

Mahatma Gandhi out of their way. I requested Chandrachudan to write all he knew about British involvement in Gandhiji's killing. And he was good enough not only to write it at some length but sign every page of the same. (I still have this signed manuscript with me.) The September 16-30, 1998, issue of *BJP Today* carried the report under the heading 'Mahatma Gandhiji's Assassination: Who Hatched the Conspiracy?'. Many national Dailies carried a summary of the report. (*The Asian Age* heading read 'BJP has new Gandhi killing theory', 18.9.1998.) Meanwhile, I started collecting information on other political murders and other mysterious happenings like the blowing up of *The Kashmir Princess* and *Kanishka* and Purulia Arms Dropping Case. A clear pattern emerged. There was a big bad foreign hand at work. This small book is a fruit of those sundry labours.

But, did this hand stop there?

Mrs. Gandhi was elected Prime Minister on January 19, 1966. Within a week—on January 24, 1966—Air India's *Kanchenjunga* blew up killing Homi Bhabha, our top nuclear scientist, and 116 others. Earlier, Bhabha had pricked the western bubble that India was too poor to go in for nuclear arms and said that if given the task he could make a Hiroshima-type A-bomb within two years for Rs. 17.5 lacs apiece. The USA had been dead opposed to India going nuclear. The US policy at the time was that scientists engaged in nuclear arms programme could be maimed or murdered to ensure "US security". Some US legislators had even requested US Intelligence agencies **not** to reveal to them such frightful things. The question, therefore, arose in many minds: was the *Kanchenjunga* crash an accident or an incident?

On December 30, 1971, Vikram Sarabhai, our top space and nuclear research man, was found dead in a hotel room

while on a visit to Thumba Equatorial Rocket Launching Station, Thiruvananthapuram. It is true a man can die suddenly. But it is also true that Sarabhai had had no history of a heart problem. Many people therefore wanted a post-mortem, to make sure there was no foul play. But Kerala Home Minister Karunakaran insisted that there shall be no post-mortem either in Thiruvananthapuram or in Ahmedabad. And he flew with the body to Gujarat, to make sure there was no post-mortem in Ahmedabad. The question arises: should the issue of post-mortem be decided by family and friends or by politicians?

On December 6, 1992, the Ayodhya structure was mysteriously demolished, as in a trice. Vijay Karan reports that "ISI celebrated the extraordinary opportunity of the occasion" and launched its "grand plan" to destabilise India. The Mumbai serial bombing followed. (vide *War By Stealth*). The matter is now sub judice. But according to Saeed Naqvi, veteran journalist, there was celebration in the Pakistan High Commission in New Delhi that evening. Why were they happy—or not unhappy—over the demolition of 'Babri Mosque'?

The December 6 incident led to demolition of scores of old temples in Pakistan. And December 6 was quoted as the reason for serial bombing in Mumbai early in 1993. Were the three incidents part of a sinister design to defame India and see to it that Hindu-Muslim and Indo-Pak relations never improved?

Is it a fact that Ghulam Ishaq Khan, then President of Pakistan, pulled up Nawaz Sharif, then Prime Minister of Pakistan, for "involvement of ISI" in the Mumbai bomb blasts in March 1993? Nawaz Sharif denied the charge but Ghulam Ishaq Khan repeated the charge (vide *The Times of India*, September 4, 1997). Was ISI alone in Mumbai bombings or did it have the blessing of its patron, the CIA?

For *The Hindu* (August 17, 2003) reported that in his first on-record interview from Saudi Arabia, Nawaz Sharif had said that 4000 Pakistani troops had lost their lives in Kargil. He also said that the mastermind of 'Kargil' (*viz.* Musharraf), instead of owning up responsibility for that 'misadventure' and resigning voluntarily, had overthrown 'the elected Government under the diktat from some "other quarters". Nawaz Sharif also threatened to "reveal all". Who could have dictated things to Pakistan Army, except the CIA and/or US Army brass?

Although Pandit Nehru talked bravely of 'Socialism', CIA was ensconced in the Prime Minister's House from day one of Independence. Some Americans connected with the Red Cross, recommended M.O. Matthai to Nehru and he promptly appointed him as his 'personal private secretary' without any clearance by the Intelligence Bureau! In this capacity Matthai controlled all the PM's steno-typists. He even came to live in the PM House. Writes Catherine Frank in her *Life of Indira Nehru Gandhi*: "For the next twelve years Matthai was like a human shield surrounding Nehru: he controlled who Nehru saw, spoke to on the phone and everything that went into or out of his office." Although Matthai claimed to hold a degree from Madras University, Nehru's biographer, S. Gopal, writes Matthai was "a stenographer with no education". Writes Catherine: "His position in the Nehru household from 1946 onwards was dangerous, and Matthai was no saint."

K. Govindan Kutty in his book, '*Seshan: An Intimate Story*', 1994, writes that "there was clearly a foreign hand" behind "the sudden outbreak and, as sudden end of the violent anti-Hindi agitation in Tamil Nadu in 1965, says Seshan."

CIA got Biju Patnaik to cooperate with it in its overflights to Tibet and incitement of Khampas. And B.K.

Nehru, our ambassador in the USA, was surprised to see President Kennedy himself greet Indian Embassy staffer Janki Ganju intimately as 'Hi Yankee'. Obviously, CIA had befriended Ganju and even introduced him to Kennedy himself!

CIA even succeeded in planting nuclear-powered devices to monitor Chinese nuclear tests in the 1960's (vide *The Times of India*, Mumbai, June 6, 2003). The whole thing is revealed in the explosive book *Spies in the Himalayas* by Capt. Mohan Singh Kohli, distinguished mountaineer.

However the most dangerous act of CIA was to break the "Hindi-Chini Bhai Bhai" relationship.

Tibet is a huge country with a distinct culture, which should have been independent. From 1912 to 1949 what little policing and post office facilities Tibet had, were manned by India. India should have got Tibet to join the UN. But Nehru quickly and thoughtlessly conceded Chinese suzerainty over Tibet. Having done that, he now decided that Thagla Ridge should come to India, though the MacMahon Line showed it on the other side! Taking a position on Tibet would have been just and right; quarrelling over Thagla Ridge made no sense. And CIA took full advantage of this silly situation to sour India-China relations.

We had no sources of information in Tibet—nor had the west—but Anglo-American Intelligence told us on the presumed basis of their superior snooping technology, that the Chinese were very weak in Tibet and one push would throw them out (vide Gen. Palit's *War in the High Himalaya*). It was under this impression that Nehru, while on his way to Colombo, said at Madras airport on October 13, 1962, that he had issued orders to "throw them out"! The immediate result was the India-China war of 1962 which hurt us badly.

Fortunately, the war did not last long. But that only

disappointed USA. Galbraith's entry in his *Ambassador's Journal* on November 21, 1962, says that U.S. pressmen were "in a bloody mood". He adds: "Many of them have come half way round the world for what looked like a very promising war. Now suddenly it had disappeared. Naturally they wanted something done about it. Half of them wanted me to advise the Indians to refuse negotiations and resume fighting. They did not say what with. The rest wanted me to throw in American troops."

It is clear USA wanted India and China to fight. That is why in 1956, they sabotaged Air India's *Kashmir Princess* by which Chou En-lai was expected to travel to Indonesia. And that is why they kept feeding us false information about Tibet. P.N. Dhar, principal private secretary to Mrs. Gandhi, reveals that Kissinger had told Foreign Secretary, T.N. Kaul (1971): "You know it would be silly for the US to favour a situation in which 800 million Chinese and 600 million Indians form a group. That would be a price that under no circumstances we would pay" (vide *India & Emergency*, p. 171). And Nehru in his naivette walked into the US trap and quarrelled with China over a wrong issue.

Galbraith's November 17 entry in his *Ambassador's Journal* says: "Incidentally, the *American Reporter*, our official propaganda sheet, has just come out with a remarkable misprint saying the purpose of our aid is to entangle India in military alliances." Assuming it was a "misprint", it correctly represented the American intention.

Senator Church (Democrat, Idaho) has said: "We respect no law save the law of the Jungle." Ambassador Moynihan wrote to Secretary of State Kissinger that Mrs. Gandhi "knows full well that we have done our share and more of bloody and dishonourable deeds." After the murder of Allende, elected President of Chile, Galbraith said, Mrs. Gandhi "wondered whether India might not be next." And

even Vajpayee cautioned the 2002 batch of IFS probationers in New Delhi on August 25, 2003: "What has happened in Iraq can happen to us, too" (vide *The Statesman*, Kolkata, August 27, 2003). Such is the menace of USA's CIA.

Allen Dulles, Chief of CIA, when his brother John Foster Dulles was US Secretary of State, said his agency had not succeeded as well in India as it had in Pakistan, but "we shall change our tactics." He added: "They had a barefoot theoretician – Gandhi – who claimed that to sincerely love a person and at the same time deceive him both in word and deed was absolutely incompatible. He was amazingly naive, but we shall make partial use of his thesis. We shall sincerely love India and at the same time sincerely deceive it. ... As we failed to take them by assault, we shall have to take them by starvation." That was the genesis of PL-480 wheat (vide *Danger of CIA* by Daljit Sen Adel, 1976).

Since the end of World War II there have been over 800 political murders. The more important of these included Diem, President of Vietnam, Allende, President of Chile, Lumumba, Prime Minister of Congo, Mujib-ur-Rehman, President of Bangladesh. According to American sources, there have been 637 attempts on the life of Castro. Earlier, there had been many attempts on the life of Nasser.

Former US Secretary of State Madeleine Albright said of former UN Secretary-General Boutros Ghali of Egypt: "I will make Boutros think I am his friend, then I will break his legs." CIA has specially specialized in causing renal cancer to its victims.

In Indonesia, CIA overthrew President Suekarno and liquidated one million people – most of them Chinese – on the plea that they were Communists. When word went round that it had been done by CIA (Central Intelligence Agency of USA) they got away with it by saying 'CIA' stood for 'Chinese Intelligence Agency'. Today, the political space cleared of Chinese and Communists, has been occupied by Islamic fundamentalists.

CIA also overthrew two leaders of Indian origin—Jagan Cheddi, President of Guyana and Mahendra Chaudhury, President of Fiji.

In 1996 Lok Sabha elections, BJP emerged as the biggest single party. The President invited BJP leader Vajpayee to form the Government. After taking the oath of office, as Shri Vajpayee was coming out, outgoing Prime Minister Narasimha Rao slipped him a note. This note said that he had tried to go nuclear but he had not succeeded. He asked Vajpayee to see if he could. Vajpayee immediately got in touch with Dr. Kalam who said he could have a nuclear test in three weeks' time. However, the President had given Vajpayee only thirteen days to prove his majority.

Before Vajpayee took office he had been negotiating with different groups. For example, Chidambaram was offered Industry and he wanted Finance. But now Rattan Sehgal, No. 2 man in the Intelligence Bureau had informed CIA that Vajpayee had decided to go nuclear. The CIA went to work and, such is its reach, that now no group was willing to come to terms with the BJP! When the Confidence Vote was being discussed, it became clear that the government had not succeeded in mustering the necessary majority. Vajpayee therefore went and tendered his resignation without waiting for the vote. That is how the first Vajpayee Government was ousted—and our nuclear programme delayed by two years.

Not content with toppling leaders and governments, CIA has not hesitated to devastate entire countries. Early in 1950, President Truman announced he was not interested in Korea and was withdrawing American troops. Koreans viewed it as American N.O.C (No Objection Certificate) to

unite North and South Korea. But as soon as the North moved in, USA said aggression had taken place. It occupied South Korea and invaded even North Korea. Obviously, the real objective was to threaten next door China in the North-East. In the fighting that ensued, 54,246 American soldiers and lacs of Koreans and Chinese got killed.

Before World War II, Vietnam was French. Japan had occupied it. After the war ended, France tried to reoccupy it. It failed. But USA now decided to occupy South Vietnam, and threaten China in the South-East. This time 58,219 US soldiers and lacs of Vietnamese got killed. At last USA had to flee the country.

Whenever a river is the dividing line between two countries, the midstream is accepted as the border. This was the case with the River Euphrates between Iran and Iraq. When Iran's Shah was a very special friend of USA, Iraq was forced to concede the entire breadth of Euphrates as the border. When, however, Iran was won by Khomeini, Iraq became a special friend of USA and it was encouraged to attack Iran. In the ten-year war that ensued, 80,000 Iraqis and 1,70,000 Iranis lost their lives.

All this warring cost millions of lives but it earned Big Business, billions of dollars. Wars meant more arms, more inventories, bigger orders, bigger profits.

In 1990, Kuwait, obviously under US inspiration, was going close to the Iraqi border and pumping out oil from the Iraqi side. Iraq was furious. In this situation, the US ambassador told Saddam that Washington was not interested in Kuwait. Later the US Under Secretary of State also told Saddam the same. However as soon as Iraq moved into Kuwait to stop the loot of its oil, USA said aggression had taken place. The Indian Ambassador in USA at the time, Mr. Abid Hussain said to the US Secretary of State Rogers that now that Saddam had been told to go back, he would

do so. But the Secretary of State told a surprised Abid, "We have taken all steps to see to it that he does NOT go back." The trick had been used to trap Saddam and land American troops next door in Saudi Arabia and keep them there. The First Gulf War ensued.

On September 11, 2001, Arab terrorists blew up World Trade Centre in New York. Without producing any evidence, USA accused Osama Bin Laden, living in Afghanistan, of organising this destruction and attacked and occupied Afghanistan. Some people see CIA hand in it. Interestingly enough, the CIA budget which was $ 36 billion during the cold war and $ 26 billion after that, has gone up so much that the US Government refuses to release the figure. Did CIA do all this to increase its budget and provide USA an excuse to attack Afghanistan and Iran – and reach out to Central Asian oil? To the question why CIA would do that to their own country, an Indian American said: "Do you think Americans are like Indians who always think of Bharat Mata?"

More recently USA accused Iraq of having weapons of mass destruction, although UN inspectors had not found any. But USA nevertheless attacked, occupied and ravaged Iraq. They caught Saddam's sons Uday and Qusay and young grandson Mustafa alive and then shot them dead. It was an act of international crime punishable by the International Court of Criminal Justice. But USA refuses to recognize that court! Writes Paul Krugman, Princeton University economist: "The natural instinct of Americans to rally round their leader in times of crisis had pushed Bush into the polling stratosphere, and his re-election seemed secure.... But Bush's advisers were greedy. They saw September 11 as an opportunity to get everything they wanted, from another round of tax cuts, to a major weakening of the Clean Air Act, to an invasion of Iraq. And

so they wrapped as much as they could in the flag... Now it has all gone wrong. The deficit is about to go above half a trillion dollars, the economy is still losing jobs, the triumph in Iraq has turned to dust and ashes... No US President has lied as much as Bush .... If you thought the last two years were bad, just wait: It's about to get worse. A lot worse." (*The New York Times*, September 13, 2003).

On May 1, 1960, a U-2 American spy plane was launched from Peshawar and headed for Sweden. Russia brought it down and held the pilot, Francis Gary Powers. And that cancelled Eisenhower-Khrushchov meeting in Paris that day. Did CIA use U-2 to sabotage that meeting?

On September 1, 1983, a South Korean civilian plane, *KE 007*, flying from New York to Seoul and carrying 269 passengers, penetrated deep into the military area of Kamachatka, Russia, for a whole hour and would neither land nor go away. In this situation Russia shot it down; it did not know that it was a civilian plane. USA cried murder. The incident killed the scheduled British, American, French and German Foreign Ministers' Conference. Was the whole thing deliberate?

In 1988 when Khomeini's Iran was having the upper hand over then US-friend Iraq, the US destroyer *Vincennes* shot down an Iranian plane carrying 290 civilians. The idea was to force Iran to stop fighting and prevent the collapse of Iraq.

Over the decades, USA has been playing so many murderous games all over the world that today if anything sinister suddenly happens anywhere, the presumption is that it is the doing of CIA, unless proved otherwise.

The irony of the situation is that the murder and mayhem USA stages abroad, it also performs at home. When President Kennedy was shot dead in 1963, an American Black intellectual said nobody need be surprised: "Murder

is as American as apple pie." And that is verily so.

Kennedy's brother, Robert Kennedy, seeking presidential election in 1968, was also shot dead. And so was Rev. Martin Luther King Jr., the most respected leader of American Blacks. And, strangely enough nobody believed the "accused murderers" to have been the actual murderers. What CIA does abroad, FBI (Federal Bureau of Investigation) does at home. Charles Lindberg was the first man to fly solo non-stop from USA to France. He became a national hero. Soon after, his 20-month son was kidnapped for ransom—and killed. Would an enormity like that happen in any other country?

USA has a population of less than thirty crores but it has twenty-five crore guns in the hands of private individuals. Most of the gunholders are white males. Every year 5 lac guns are stolen. Gunfire is the biggest single cause of death among young blacks. Only 2 per cent guns are used against intruders. The remaining 98 per cent of the times, residents accidentally shoot a loved one or themselves—or the burglars take the gun and kill them with it. (vide *Stupid White Men* by Michael Moore, distinguished writer and filmmaker). But the gun lobby is so powerful, and the gun culture so popular, that the US legislature dare not ban or even regulate gun trade! For this and other reasons, crime rate is the highest in USA—and about the lowest in India. USA with a population of less than thirty crores has twenty-one lacs in jail; India with a population of more than a hundred crores, has only three lacs in jail, a majority of them only undertrials.

On top of this, US leaders don't hesitate to self-destruct their society. Democratic President Johnson had got mired in Vietnam. College students all over the States had been shouting: "Hey, Hey! How many kids did you kill today?" He desperately wanted to meet Vietnamese leaders to find

a face-saving way out. "If I could just get into a room with Ho Chi Minh, we could settle this thing."

But peace in Vietnam in 1968 would have ensured Johnson's re-election. In this situation his rival Nixon's men reached Vietnam leaders with the word that they could get better terms from a Republican regime. And so the murderous war was allowed to continue for more years.

A similar treachery was witnessed in 1980, when Democratic Carter was President. Iran had taken American Embassy staff as hostages. After some time Iran was willing to relent. But that would have ensured a second term for Carter. And that did not suit Republican candidate Reagan. And so his lieutenant, Kissinger, conveyed to Iran that they could expect better terms from them. And that continued the hostage crisis for months more.

So much for American patriotism! No wonder only 23 per cent Americans are proud of their culture (vide U.S. based Pew Global Attitudes Project headed by Madeleine Albright, former US Secretary of State.) The figures are 74 per cent for India, 63 per cent for Bangladesh, 50 per cent for Pakistan, 21 per cent for China and just 9 per cent for UK (vide *The Hindustan Times*, June 8, 2003).

The world looks at USA and is at once enthralled and alarmed. Samuel Johnson, king of English prose, had said: "I am willing to love all mankind, **except an American.**" And Oscar Wilde wrote in his play *A Woman of No Importance*: 1893, Act I:

Mrs. Allonhy: They say, Lady Hunstanton, that when good Americans die, they go to Paris."

Lady Hunstanton: Indeed? And when bad Americans die, where do they go?

Lord Illingworth: Oh, they go to America."

Charlie Chaplin said of US justice: "American law is such, if Government is against you, you're sunk, even if you are completely innocent." He therefore left USA. That is how they tortured our Rajneesh.

Neville Chamberlain, British Prime Minister, when World War II broke out in 1939, said: "It is always best and safest to count on nothing from the Americans except words."

Writer Christopher Isherwood has said: "In USA, 'Sympathy' is in the dictionary, and everything else is available in the drug store."

And Will Durant, historian of world civilizations, says: "How can we take America seriously with its two centuries of civilization, while that of China is five thousand years old? (*Pleasures of Philosophy*, p. 351).

The question is: Why is America what it is? Why is there so much ignorance and arrogance, crime and violence, in USA?

Reason No. 1 is that USA was born in violence. The Europeans who came here cut down forests, shot down birds and animals (bison and illango) and liquidated whole native populations. Destruction became inbuilt in the American psyche. Perhaps there has not been a greater tragedy in world history than the genocide of Red Indians. Here were innocent, fine, honourable tribes, very much like our Santhals and Gonds. The white man introduced Gun, Rum and Pox (from small-pox to venereal diseases) that destroyed American Indian society. The white slogan was: 'The only good Indian is the dead Indian'. And before long they were all dead—or confined to reservations, as though they were so much cattle.

They have no vote, no passport.

Helen Hunt Jackson has done a study of how the Whites signed treaty after treaty with the Indians, only to violate the same at the first opportunity. *A Century of Dishonour* covers this infamy from the American War of Independence

onwards. And this violence was reflected even in the American Civil War. Although USA had a population of only three crores at the time, more than five lacs—5,62,130—died and 4,18,201 were wounded in that war!

A second factor in American history is the composition of its population. Other countries have a geography, a settled society, a history, a tradition, a set of tried and tested values. USA had neither. The whole country was a kind of Wild West, with the law of the jungle as the only law. *The New York Times* writes "The world sees menace in American values."

It is generally believed that most of the Americans came from England. The fact that the two countries speak the same language strengthens this belief. But facts are otherwise. According to the 1990 US census, 19.6 per cent Americans reported German ancestry, 13.1 per cent Irish, only 11 per cent English. And Italians and Blacks were not far behind. Actually until World War I, sentiment in USA was strongly anti-British. Apart from the 1770's War of Independence, in 1812, British troops from Canada had invaded USA and burnt down the White House in Washington. During the Civil War, Britain and France were seriously thinking of recognizing the seceding Southern Confederacy. And during World War I, British jobs to thousands of unemployed American youths turned the sentiment against Germany and for England.

Lincoln had White, Black, Turk and Portuguese blood in him. Roosevelts are Dutch (the earlier name of New York was New Amsterdam). And President Teddy Roosevelt loudly thanked God that he had "not one drop of British blood in him". The Kennedys are Irish, sworn enemies of the English. Eisenhower was German. And for leading economist, Lord Keynes, "The only really sympathetic and original thing in America is the niggers who are charming."

This hotch-potch society has produced a cocktail of a culture. Although the American currency declares 'In God We trust', the only god they have is the almighty Dollar. Many of them even say: "God is dead".

This situation bred 'Robber Barons', with Rockefeller saying "God gave me my money".

President after president made no bones about it. The business of America, they said, is 'Business'. "Corporations", said Lincoln, "have been enthroned. An era of corruption in high places will follow." Hayes said: "It is a Government of the corporations, for the corporations and by the corporations." "Corporations", writes Lord Thurlow, "have neither bodies to be punished, nor souls to be condemned; they, therefore, do as they like." And these corporations cheated right, left and middle. The American railway system was built with loans from Europe. And none of these debts were repaid—not to talk of interest!

Presidents Roosevelt and Eisenhower both complained of the Industrial military complex ruling America. Here Generals retire and become Vice-Presidents of big business houses. There is no countervailing force against the coalition of Big Business and Army. Politicians are only brokers of power.

USA is not ruled by its president of its legislature, the Congress. It is ruled by Pentagon the Defence Department. No wonder this HQ of US Defence is the biggest building in the World. It is five times the size of Capitol, the US Congress building. Legislators are kept happy with defence factories in their constituencies to provide jobs for their constituents—and of course with generous donations for their re-election. The President is a creature of this military-industrial complex.

This military-industrial complex uses the military and economic power of USA to gobble up the economies of other

countries in the name of globalization. The WTO (World Trade Organisation) has been variously described as West's Trade Organisation and even World Terrorist Organisation. They use the UN, the World Bank and the International Monetary Fund—all of them located in USA!—to control world economics and world politics to their advantage. And in the booming name of liberalization, these institutions have drained $43 billion from Russia to the West in the first ten years alone. This is the reality.

In September 1963, Secretary of State Dean Rusk called on USSR Foreign Minister Gromyko in New York. He told him they will go out for a drive—obviously because his residence would be bugged. After this drive, while walking around, Rusk told him that Kennedy very much wanted to improve US-USSR relations. He said: "Something serious is afoot" and "Kennedy is thinking of reducing US forces in Europe." Soon after—on November 22, 1963—Kennedy was shot dead. (vide Gromyko's *Memoirs*, p. 137).

Dobrynin, Russian ambassador in USA, reports that Jackie Kennedy told him and Mikoyan, with tears in her eyes, that on the very morning of assassination, Kennedy had told her that he had decided to make up with Russia. But the industrial-military complex would have none of it. So Kennedy was bumped off.

Khrushchev in Russia was thinking in similar terms. When the Russian military asked for funds to build a big navy, Khrushchev asked them: Can you ever face the American Navy? Will not the Russian navy be bottled up in port? He therefore refused funds. Soon after—in October 1964—Khrushchev was removed as the First Secretary of the Soviet Union. He was replaced by Brezhnev, who conceded all the demands of the Russian military establishment. The military complex in Russia toed the line of the American industrial-military complex.

Writes Gromyko in his *Memoirs*: "Was it accident that history almost simultaneously moved both reformers from the stage?" He adds: "No answer exists for such questions and history does not accept conjecture." (pp. 137 & 274). However, if you put two and two together it is clear that the American industrial-military complex removed Kennedy—and the Russian military dislodged Khrushchev.

The break-up of USSR and the signing of WTO was a victory for the West, the United States, the MNCs. The World, said Brooke Adams, is "at our feet". But action and reaction are equal and opposite. Already we have a situation of the West (Anglo-America) virtually versus the Rest (of the World). The isolation of USA over Iraq is complete. From Seattle to Cancun there is a revolt against Big Business, WTO, IMF and World Bank.

Everybody likes to be liked. But today the USA is feared and hated. People have come to disbelieve whatever USA says or does. Today people even question the American claim to have landed Armstrong on the moon. Philippe Lheureux has done a whole book in French—*La Nasa a-t-ella menti*? asking, among other things—why the flag was seen fluttering when there is no air on the moon? And Gingrich, erstwhile Speaker of the US House of Representatives, says: "No society can survive, no civilization can survive, with 12-year olds having babies, with 15-year olds killing each other, with 17-year olds dying of AIDS, with 18-year olds getting Diplomas they can't read."

At one time the National Association for the Advancement of Coloured People, the leading organization of American Blacks had wanted to invite Gandhiji to USA. But they soon realized: "This land is not civilized enough to receive a coloured man as an honoured guest." And only recently (January 24, 2003), *Maxim* magazine in an alleged 'humor' article headlined "Maxim's Kick-Ass Workout",

depicted a strapping man in a muscle T-shirt beating up an image of Gandhi. The article, attempting to show how fighting can bring fitness, calls for "a healthy regimen of violent assaults" and urges readers to "teach those pacifists a lesson about aggression." The three page article includes 21 different scenes of the man "hitting, choking and throwing Gandhi... ."

So this is America. No wonder only 23 per cent Americans are proud of America. Today, even USA is making fun of its President, selling "Bush dolls in all his poses". After the collapse of USSR, American humorist Michel Moore had said: "One evil empire down, one to go." Is the American century already coming to an end? What next?

Om Shanti!

□

Netaji Subhas Chandra Bose

The Indian Freedom Movement threw up a whole galaxy of leaders. In this galaxy Subhas Chandra Bose stood out as a comet. If he had been around at the time of transfer of power in 1946-47, there would probably have been no Partition, and he, rather than Nehru, would have emerged as Prime Minister. But powerful forces bent upon partitioning India saw him 'safely' eliminated in 1945. What happened? And how? And why?

Subhas was born in 1897. While still at school, he was thrilled to the "marrow of my bones" by the teachings of Swami Vivekananda. Here was a man with a spiritual bent of mind dedicated to social service: *'Atmano mokshartham jagadhitaya'* (salvation of self and service of humanity).

Subhas qualified for ICS but he did not join the service, promptly resigned and plunged in the Freedom Movement. Here Deshbandhu Chittaranjan Das, another titan of the Freedom Movement, saw in Subhas the hero of tomorrow and started grooming him for leadership. In Alipore Jail, Das instructed Subhas in metaphysics and moral philosophy. When Das became Mayor of Calcutta (about the same time Nehru became Chairman, Allahabad Municipal Committee and Sardar Patel, Chairman Ahmedabad Municipal Committee) he appointed Subhas

Chief Executive Officer. Here Subhas donated half of his salary to social service. Das even worked out a Hindu-Muslim Pact in Bengal in 1923. When Deshbandhu passed away prematurely in 1925, the Congress conferred all his offices—the Triple Crown of Mayor Calcutta, Bengal Provincial Congress Committee President and leader Swarajist Party in the State Assembly—to J. Sen Gupta. And when Sen Gupta passed away, the Triple Crown was transferred to the Gandhian P.C. Ghosh. Subhas was by-passed.

Meanwhile, the British saw in Subhas an uncompromising nationalist and packed him off to the notorious Mandalay Jail in Burma. Mandalay had ruined the health of Lokmanya Tilak and Lala Lajpat Rai, and now it ruined the health of Subhas. He was kept in the same cell with a TB patient, and Subhas soon developed incipient TB.

In a brief span of 48 years, Subhas spent nine years in jail, three years in forced exile (he was packed off to Europe straight from jail, and not allowed to see even his dying father) and four years struggling for Indian Independence in Germany and the Far East. In the interregnum, he worked on the All Party Motilal Nehru Committee which produced the famous Nehru Report for Constitutional Reform.

In 1938 Subhas was elected the Congress President. During his term, he set up a Planning Board under the Chairmanship of Nehru, condemned Japanese invasion of China and sent a medical team, led by Dr. Kotnis, to serve the Chinese people.

In 1939, Subhas again stood for Congress Presidency (Nehru had also just had two consecutive terms in 1936 and 1937)—and won it. And that put the fat in the fire. The Tripuri Congress adopted the Pant resolution asking

Subhas to nominate his Working Committee in consultation with Mahatma Gandhi. But Congress stalwarts Nehru, Patel, Rajendra Prasad, C. Rajagopalachari resigned and would not work with him. Gandhiji therefore advised him to form his own committee, or resign, and let the AICC elect a new President. In this situation, Subhas resigned and formed the Forward Bloc. (He met Savarkar and Jinnah in June 1940. And he told Jinnah that if he joined hands with Hindus he would be the first Prime Minister of Independent India). And then he quietly slipped out of India on Jan. 16, 1941 through the British tentacles–even as Shivaji had escaped from Aurangzeb's jail in Agra.

The whole thing was less than fair to Subhas. If Gandhiji - and Patel and Nehru and others - did not want Subhas for a second term, they could have said so - and prevented his re-election. But having allowed a free contest, in which Pattabhi Sitaramayya was backed by the Congress Chief Ministers in seven provinces - it was hardly fair to deny Subhas his office and subvert his Presidency.

Nor was that all. Gandhiji chose exactly the dates of Tripuri Congress to go on a five-day fast on the relatively minor issue of an elected Assembly for the princely State of Rajkot. He thereby diverted all the attention away from Subhas and Tripuri, and to himself in Rajkot. Subhas was running high temperature, and some Gandhians chose to dub Subhas' medical and nursing team as 'Calcutta's *Natak Mandali*'.

Why did Subhas' relations not work out with Gandhi, Nehru and Patel? The basic reason was that all these leaders had a different background and they were facing big and complex issues.

It was World War II and public sentiment was anti-British - and even pro-German. In the beginning, Gandhi was for unconditional support to the war effort and most other leaders were opposed to it. (In Egypt Nahas Pasha's Wafd Party followed this course, and was wiped out by public opinion). Later, in 1942, Gandhiji came out for struggle against the British, and Nehru, Azad, C.R. and many other leaders were opposed to it. Resignation of Congress ministries in 1939 and launching of 'Quit India' Movement in 1942 made the British anti-Hindu and caused them to support the Muslim League demand for Partition. We tried to sit on two stools - and fell betwixt the two!

Even otherwise, in this complex situation differences of opinion and assessment were inevitable. Subhas apart, Gandhi and Nehru had serious differences, Nehru and Patel had even more serious differences; why, even Patel and Gandhi had serious differences particularly in 1946-47.

With the demise of Lokmanya Tilak, C.R. Das and Lala Lajpat Rai, power in the Congress shifted away from Maharashtra, Bengal and Punjab, and went to the Hindi area, Madras, Gujarat and Bombay. Bengal, particularly, felt alienated.

Sardar Patel was closest to Gandhiji. And he did not approve of Subhas - or Bengal Congress - taking a different, non-Gandhian line. Relations between Sardar and Subhas further soured when the former's elder brother Vithal Bhai Patel, joined hands with the latter in Geneva and, on May 9, 1933, issued a joint manifesto saying: "As a political leader Mahatma Gandhi has failed. The time has therefore come for a radical reorganisation of the Congress on a new principle and with a new method."

(Vithal Bhai, who had been Speaker of the Central Assembly, was a very independent minded person. He once said to Gandhiji to his face: "*Tame bhool kidhi; tame moorakh chho*" (You made that mistake. You are a fool). Gandhiji left the room and never again saw him. Vithal Bhai also resented that his younger brother Vallabh Bhai, was made

Congress President, in 1931, but not he).

And then Vithal Bhai willed Rs. 1,20,000 – a princely sum in those days – to Subhas "for any foreign propaganda that he may decide upon for the uplift of India." Gandhiji complimented Subhas on his "magnificent and devoted nursing of Vithal Bhai at much risk to his own health". However, Vallabh Bhai challenged his brother's Will on the ground that it had been signed by an ailing Vithal Bhai on the last day of his life and that it had not been countersigned by any doctor. The case was argued for Vallabh Bhai by Bhulabhai Desai, and for Subhas by R.R. Das, brother of C.R. Das. The court decided in favour of Sardar Patel. Patel-Bose relations soured further.

Nehru-Subhas relations were never smooth. Writes S.K. Patil: "Subhas could make friends easily; not Jawaharlal. They clashed whenever they met. Jawaharlal would not like Subhas in the Working Committee, nor would Subhas Chandra acknowledge Jawaharlal's supremacy."

Apart from personal rivalry, Nehru's socialism was derived from Marxism; Subhas' from Vivekananda. When Dilip Kumar Roy, an old friend and Aurobinda Shishya, drew Subhas' attention to criticism of religion in Nehru's autobiography, his response was: "Leave him alone. What have I in common with him ideologically?"

Subhas' relations with Gandhi were at once complex and variable. Due to Gandhiji's preference for Gandhians in Bengal leadership, Subhas felt by-passed and neglected. He did not approve of Gandhiji's loin cloth. For long years Bengal was given an ad-hoc Congress Committee. The 1930 Salt Satyagrah in Calcutta consisted of a lone Gandhian reading a prescribed book at a city crossing!

After the 1936 General elections, Bose wanted Congress to join hands with Fazlul Haq's Krishak Mazdoor Party, give the State a stable Hindu-Muslim coalition. Gandhiji

agreed. But under the influence of Maulana Azad and G.D. Birla, Gandhiji reversed his position. Maulana was of the view that in a Muslim-majority province Muslim League should be allowed to form the government. And Birla saw business interest in a League led government backed by British business interests and Nalini Ranjan Sarkar, a former Congress leader who had joined hands with them. (Four years later Dr. Syama Prasad Mookerji joined hands with Haq and gave Bengal a Hindu-Muslim coalition, but that was too late to stop Bengal's drift to partition.) According to Nirad Chaudhari, Birla feared that a Hindu-Muslim coalition of Congress and Haq would hurt Marwari business interests (*Thy Hand, Great Anarch*, p. 486).

While on occasions Gandhiji addressed Subhas coldly as 'Dear Friend' and told Patel he was "not at all dependable", in the same vein he also said that "there is nobody, but he who can be President". On another occasion he described him as "a patriot of patriots". After the Tripuri dust had settled, Gandhiji wrote to him on 13.11.1939, "For the time being you are my lost sheep. Some day I shall find you returning to the fold, if I am right and my love is pure."

Basically, Gandhi-Subhas differences were religio-cultural rather than personal. As Nirad Chaudhari put it: "The Bengali Hindus belonged to two schools of Hinduism, the Saktas, or those who worshipped power in the Mother Goddess, and the Vaishnavas, or those who were followers of Krishna, and practised non-violence. Now, the higher castes of Bengalis who were the social element behind nationalism, were overwhelmingly Sakta and therefore no believers in non-violence. They even despised Vaishnava non-violence, and all the more so because the Vaishnavas of Bengal were overwhelmingly traders. The followers of Gandhiji in Bengal were mostly Vaishnavas, to whom his doctrines would naturally appeal." (*Thy Hand Great Anarch*,

p. 290) Gandhiji was a Vaishnava, Subhas a Sakta. It was a case of two very different wave-lengths. Gandhiji didn't have this problem with Nehru, who had no religious conviction of any kind.

Subhas overcame his old antipathies and named two of the INA regiments after Nehru and Patel (and he was the first to hail Gandhiji as "The Father of the Nation"). But Nehru continued his animus against Subhas. He had said that he would go out and fight Subhas if he entered the country with the Japanese, when there were no Japanese in INA. But he promptly appropriated Subhas' slogan 'Jai Hind'. At the time of INA trial of Shah Nawaz, Prem Sehgal and G.S. Dhillon in the Red Fort, he appeared in a black lawyer's gown because it was a great 'photo opportunity'. But he refused to rehabilitate INA soldiers or even give them pension. Netaji's pictures were taboo in post-Independence Indian cantonments.

Shri Shyamlal Jain, steno of Asaf Ali, who was Secretary to INA Defence Committee during those days in 1945-46, told the Khosla Commission that Nehru dictated to him a letter addressed to Mr. Attlee, Prime Minister of Britain, saying "I understand from a reliable source that Subhas Chandra Bose, your war criminal, has been allowed to enter Russia. This is a clear case of treachery on the part of Russia. Please take note of it and do the needful."

After the war even Indian soldiers who had fought INA in the North-East were charmed by the INA ideology. They called on Gandhiji, who told them: "I know there is a new ferment and a new awakening among all the ranks today. Not a little of the credit for this awakening is due to Netaji Bose."

As these soldiers took Bapu's leave, they sought his permission to shout some slogans which they readily got. And they repeatedly shouted 'Jai Hind', 'Netaji ki Jai'.

Netaji's 27,000-strong INA was not - and could not possibly be - a military success. But it was a terrific psychological success. It triggered the Naval Mutiny. The whole thing made early Independence inevitable. But before all this could materialise, Subhas had to go through fire.

Uttamchand Malhotra and Bhagat Ram Talwar helped him escape to Afghanistan as 'Ziauddin'. But Kabul was a regular snake-pit and he had to bribe his way to Russia where no senior person would see him for fear of Britain. And Subhas was too independent minded to tow the Soviet line. He disapproved of Russian invasion of Finland. Subhas left India on Jan. 16, 1941 but he was able to reach Berlin only on April 2, 1941. He was able to meet Ribbentrop, Foreign Minister of Germany, only on Nov. 29, 1941. And he could meet Hitler only on May 28, 1942. There were many reasons for these unconscionable delays.

Hitler was not interested in Indian Independence. He thought it alright for Britain to rule India. In his post-dinner 'Table Talk', he repeatedly said that Britain had become great because it held India; Germany, he said, could also become great, only if it had an India of its own in Ukraine, which was part of USSR. Hence the German attack on Russia. Bose wholly disapproved of the invasion of Russia.

Italy and Japan wanted a Tripartite announcement with Germany for the independence of India. But Hitler refused. Subhas on his part refused to speak on German radio unless Germany supported Indian independence and recognised an emigre Free Government of India. It was only after Cripps Mission, which promised part transfer of power, but which also conceded the principle of Partition, that Subhas agreed to speak on German radio, to urge rejection of these proposals.

After his meeting with Hitler, Subhas told his friends that Hitler was like the Faqir of Ipi, with whom rational

dialogue was not possible. In the winter of 1942, Subhas told Admiral Conoris of Germany: "You know as well as I do that Germany cannot now win this war."

Nor was that all. German Foreign Office had any number of pro-British elements. Some of them (Black Orchestra) were later found involved in an attempt on Hitler's life. They didn't want Subhas. They even suggested that Subhas move to a neutral country like Switzerland. Subhas in Germany never felt that there was ground beneath his feet!

In June 1942, Italy was willing to fly Subhas straight from Rhodes to Rangoon. And in July 1942 Italy actually carried out such a flight. But Germany said that Italy could not be trusted with security and safety. They now put him on a U-boat in which Subhas could sit at the table or lie down in beds but he could not stand up. It was a three months' hazardous journey after thirteen months wasted in Germany.

Subhas had told Oshima Hiroshi, the Japanese envoy in Berlin, that Germans wanted to keep him in Germany to surrender him later to the British who were 'itching' to capture him. Near Madagascar, Subhas was transferred to a Japanese submarine. And after another month under the sea, he was at last in the East. Once in Japan, Subhas took over the INA from Rash Behari Bose and Mohan Singh, roused Indian civilians and soldiers alike, and set up Azad Hind government which was duly recognised by Japan, Germany, Italy, Ireland, Burma, Croatia and Nanking.

Although India was never part of Japan's plan for an East Asian co-prosperity sphere and its half-hearted Imphal Expedition was planned months before Subhas reached Japan, the British in India were terrified. They did not dare to use Indian soldiers against Germans at El Alamein in North Africa. And they concentrated all their forces in the mouth of the Hooghly, leaving just one Brigade in Assam.

British agents, however, played even more havoc in South East Asia than in Germany. Subhas and Burma's Ba Maw said they had to face British forces in the open and "the hidden enemy behind, within and around."

Japan had banked on a short war with quick victory. But UK and USA were far away from Japan, and they were not easily beaten on sea. More. Japan did not have enough oil for a long war and it did not have shipping enough to import oil. Therefore, long before the American bombardment of Japan, Subhas told his cabinet in October 1944 that Japan had as good as lost the war.

The actual surrender of Japan came on August 15, 1945. And on August 23, Radio Japan announced the death of Subhas in an air crash on August 18. The news was too sudden and too sad to be taken as true. Gandhiji and Malaviyaji said there should be no *shraadh* unless the news was confirmed. For the same reason Congress did not condole his death. It was widely believed that Subhas must have escaped to Russia. However, this could not be true. For one thing, Subhas never had any friendly relations with USSR or with CPI. Even when he escaped from India, he was only quietly allowed to go to Germany through Russian territory; he was not met by any Russian of any importance. Before Japan surrendered USSR had declared war on it. There was, therefore, no question of Russia letting Subhas cross over from the Japanese side. Earlier the Russian envoy in Tokyo refused to accept Netaji's letter. In any case Russia would have never risked British displeasure over giving shelter to Subhas, their Enemy No. 1.

Subhas no doubt was right in foreseeing a split between Russia and the West. But he was not realistic in expecting it to happen that soon. And now that Subhas' family also agrees with his closest colleague, Habibur Rehman, and

with the concerned doctors, that he died in that crash, it has to be accepted as a fact. A man like Subhas cannot hide – or be hidden – anywhere on earth for half a century and more. However many other questions have also been raised about the authenticity of the crash report: why was the death announced five days after the event? Did the crash take place at the northern end or the southern end of the air field? Did Subhas and other passengers have proper seats or did they squat on the floor of the plane? Why are there conflicting reports about cremation on August 21, 22 or 23? Why was Habib not allowed to see the body—and attend the cremation? Why is there no photograph? Why was there no inquiry into the crash?

All these are legitimate questions. But considering the confusion and chaos following defeat in war, all these contradictions can be explained as due to general grief and bewilderment.

However a bigger question is whether the crash of August 18 was an accident or a contrived incident. According to Habibur Rehman, after running about three fourths of the runway, the plane made a steep take off, almost vertically. The plane circled over the airport and within a few seconds the plane nose-dived and crashed to the ground. And according to Lt. Col. Sakai, another eyewitness, "I saw the rear wheel break away.... The propeller of the left engine fell out and then the engine itself broke off and the plane crashed."

Why should a bomber take off vertically, as if it were a helicopter? And why should the wheel, the propeller and the engine fly off? One is reminded of an old circus trick in which a car comes honking in and then, within minutes, the wheels, the hood, the engine, everything comes off!

According to a panel of experts, "For a two-engined bomber, it was physically impossible to make a steep ascent immediately after take-off." It concluded: "In the entire Japanese air conditions before and during the pacific war there did not occur any other case of propeller falling out during take-off."

It is clear the plane did not crash; it was made to crash. Obviously it was one of those Kamikaze ('divine winds' i.e. suicide) operations – for reasons of state.

All through the war, Americans had been saying they would hang the Mikado (Emperor Hirohito) of Japan. Geobbels also says in his diaries that USA wanted to try Hirohito as a 'War criminal'. But at the and of it they did not so much as touch Hirohito. And they allowed him to continue Emperor of Japan! There is no charity in politics, and certainly not in war time.

If we put two and two together it is clear that there was a deal between Japan and Anglo-Americans. They spared Hirohito and asked in return the liquidation of Subhas. And Japan was not in a position to say no. According to the Russian *History of Diplomacy*, "In the spring-summer of 1945 the Japanese communicated with the Anglo-Saxon powers through three neutral countries: Sweden, Switzerland and Portugal."

Although Japan had the greatest respect for Subhas and Prime Minister Tojo described him as the "greatest revolutionary" and "greatest hero", it was helpless in the new situation of defeat and surrender. Allied Radio was threatening more Hiroshimas unless Subhas was surrendered dead or alive.

Subhas, therefore, was denied the use of his special plane. He was angry. In a letter he dictated to his secretary Bhaskaran at 3 a.m. on August 17, for his cabinet colleague Thivy, he said that he might be involved in an air crash. Obviously he smelt a crash in the air. His colleagues begged of him to take some rest and Subhas only smiled and said:

"I shall have enough time to rest from to-morrow." It was to be a rest for good.

Only publication of secret Japan-Allied negotiations in the spring and summer of 1945 can throw light on what exactly happened on August 18. UK is going to sit on its papers at least upto 2021. And 293 million pages of American Intelligence are yet to be declassified; and 93 million pages have already been exempted from publication by Clinton's Executive Order. In the absence of a complete record, and on a balance of circumstances, Subhas must be presumed to have been eliminated, unless proved otherwise. Ominously enough, even the inquiries made by Lord Wavell, Viceroy, Lord Mountbatten and Gen. Mac Arthur of USA have not seen the light of the day. Obviously they have much to hide.

National interest demanded a comprehensive inquiry into the circumstances of the death/disappearance of Subhas. And the best person to do so would have been Justice Radha Binod Pal who had served on the Japanese War Crimes Tribunal and won Japan's hearts. But the then Government of India would not do the obvious. When, however, a non-official inquiry by Justice Pal was mooted, Mr. Nehru appointed Mr. Shah Nawaz for the purpose. Mr. Shah Nawaz not only had no judicial experience, he was a Congress Minister. And he was directed by Mr. Nehru **not** to visit Taiwan, the scene of the disaster. His report did not satisfy the people. And so over 350 MPs demanded a second inquiry. And the man now selected was Justice Khosla, who was such a favourite with the Congress. He had already presided over thirteen Commissions! This gentleman described Netaji as a 'puppet', 'pawn' and 'quisling'. Small wonder his report carried no conviction. He used the material of this report to do a book *The Last Days of Netaji* even before submitting the report. And he specially spent an extra day in Taiwan to buy a gift for Mrs. Gandhi. Here was a judge who was anything but judicious. It is against this background that the present (NDA) Government has appointed a third Commission to probe the matter.

General Fuziwara, Chief of Japan's War-time Intelligence (Hikari Kikan) has said: "Why the Japanese will discredit their war-time national leaders? It is for the Indian Parliament to find out what happened to (Subhas) Chandra Bose." However, neither the Indian Parliament nor the Indian Judges can unravel the mystery unless Japan, UK and USA come out with the facts. And if they fail to do so, the presumption would be that they have much to hide. Meanwhile, New Delhi could ask for the findings of the three Commissions appointed by Wavell, Mountbatten and Mac Arthur.

The country is entitled to know the truth, the whole truth and nothing but the truth.

□

Why Did the British Want Gandhi Out?

It is for England to explain the mysterious presence of two camera-carrying Englishmen from the British High Commission, then opposite Birla House, at Gandhiji's prayer meeting in New Delhi on the fatal January 30, 1948. But the lay reader would be curious to know why exactly the British wanted Gandhiji out of the Indian scene. After all the British had wanted India partitioned; the Congress and even Gandhiji, had acquiesced. And Partition was a fact in January 1948.

Well, yes and no. Although India had been partitioned and millions had left their homes, most of the refugees thought they would be back home in a few weeks or months, when tempers cooled down.

Mr. Jinnah, as a brilliant lawyer, had won the political case for Partition, but he had lost the country. He was appalled by the carnage that followed. Sarojini Naidu, who had been very close to him, had once remarked that Jinnah was a great lawyer and a great leader but he was blissfully ignorant of history, literature and philosophy. He had not realised that cutting up of an organic unity like the Indian State in 1947 would inevitably lead to large-scale bloodshed.

In Lahore, even Chief Minister Mamdot was beseiged by angry Muslim refugees from Amritsar screaming for his blood: "*Jaan lenay aye hain, jaan lekay jaenge*" —we have come to take (his) life; and we will go only when we have taken it.—(vide Shaukat Hayat's *A Nation That Lost Its Soul*, p. 136.) It was in the hope of "neutralising some of the despair of millions of homeless destitute Muslim refugees" that Jinnah made a bid for Kashmir, says J.N. Sahni, former Editor *The Hindustan Times* in his book *The Lid Off* (p. 290). (Incidentally, in 1965, Ayub also launched the war to divert attention from the Presidential Election that he had rigged against Miss Fatima Jinnah).

In Karachi, Jinnah was shocked to see Muslim refugees sack the city of his birth. He told M.A. Khuhro, Chief Minister of Sindh: "Don't you think we have become independent twenty years too soon?" Later, when the looters in Karachi were fired upon, the refugees promptly dubbed him, 'Qatil-e-Azam' (The Great Killer).

Dr. (Col.) Elahi Bux, who was looking after the ailing Mr. Jinnah at Ziarat, Baluchistan - and who has done the book *The Last Days of the Quaid-e-Azam* - told Mohammed Yahya Khan, Education Minister of NWFP, that Mr. Jinnah once told Liaqat Ali, Prime Minister, that he had committed the "biggest blunder" of his life in creating Pakistan and would like to go to Delhi and tell Nehru to forget the "follies of the past and become friends again" (vide *The Times of India*, September 11, 1988).

Nor was that all. When I visited Pakistan in February 1999, Mr. Mahmud Kasuri, a leading citizen of Lahore, whose grand-father had been President Punjab Provincial Congress Committee, told me something that surprised me. Some time after Partition, Miss Fatima Jinnah, sister of Mr. Jinnah, asked Mrs. Iftikharuddin—her husband, Ifti had been PPCC President and later Punjab Muslim League

President—for a good cook. Mrs. Ifti wondered why they needed a cook when they had the whole Government House, Karachi to themselves. And Miss Jinnah said they wanted one for their Delhi residence! Obviously Mr. Jinnah was thinking in terms of visiting Delhi and residing in his Delhi house on a regular basis.

This being the thinking at Mr. Jinnah's end the British were obviously afraid that a Gandhi visit to Pakistan could mark the beginning of the end of Partition—and of the hatreds that had culminated in Partition. "The best laid schemes of mice and men"—and even of Mountbattens!—as poet Robert Burns would put it, could still go away. Mountbatten had played dirty by fast forwarding Attlee's date of transfer of power from June 1948 to August 1947, when Jinnah was dying of T.B., and Mountbatten himself admitted that if Jinnah had died before Partition, there would have been no Partition. "If in fact, Jinnah had died, literally before the transfer of power (since) he was the only, I repeat the only, stumbling block.... The others were not so obdurate.... I am sure the Congress would have found some compromise with them, and there would have been no Partition." (vide Lapierre & Collins: *Mountbatten and the Partition of India*, p. 40). Fact is that the British establishment had decided on Partition as an imperial necessity. King George VI and Churchill had both told Mountbatten to "Keep a bit of India, keep a bit of India".

Writes Dr. Ajeet Jawed: "After agreeing to divide, Jinnah met Mountbatten again and said that he did not want Pakistan but would be content with an honourable settlement with the Congress and the British Government for a United India. Mountbatten snubbed Jinnah and said it was too late to think of an alternative." And Jinnah was too proud to publicly admit his blunder. The dye of Partition was cast. (*Secular and Nationalist Jinnah*, p. 279.)

And now Mountbatten played another trick. Gandhiji had decided to go on fast on January 13 for general improvement in Hindu-Muslim relations. Earlier, the Government of India had decided to withhold a sum of Rs. 55 crores only from Pakistan because of its incursion into Kashmir. Nehru had told the House: "We are not going to provide for sinews of war against us in Kashmir." It was Mountbatten who called on Gandhiji on the first morning of the fast and asked him to make the payment of Rs. 55 crores to Pakistan a pre-condition for breaking his fast. He admitted to Larry Collins and Dominique Lapierre, "I was the man who suggested the Rs. 55 crores to Gandhiji who had not even heard of it" (vide *Mountbatten & Partition*, p. 50). (However Mountbatten's Press Secretary, Alan Campbell Johnson says in *Mission with Mountbatten* that on January 12 Gandhiji had met Mountbatten and sought his opinion about Rs. 55 crores. Who is speaking the truth? Mountbatten or his secretary?) Now, therefore, under the pressure of Bapu's fast, the Government went back on its own Rs. 55 crore decision. This infuriated the people. Mountbatten had no business to set up Gandhi against a decision taken by the Cabinet, including Nehru and Patel, and thus make him a target of people's wrath.

However, the whole thing fitted into the British scheme of things, namely, to partition India and to get rid of Gandhiji who was the leader most opposed to it.

Gandhiji's creed of *Ahimsa* had no doubt freed the British from the fear of the revolutionary. Earlier, even the rustling of tree leaves would make many Englishmen think that there was probably a terrorist hiding up there! However, Gandhiji had also roused and galvanised the Indian masses. And the British establishment could not forget or forgive that. Churchill not only kept on asking why Gandhi had not died yet, he refused to see him anywhere, any-time.

Nor was that all. After Partition, Gandhiji said he saw darkness all around. He had serious ideological differences with Nehru. Throughout the thirties Nehru used to say, "We must oppose the Wardha Line." And now Gandhiji told him in his letter in Hindustani on October 5, 1945, "The first thing I want to write about is the difference of outlook between us. If the difference is fundamental, then I feel the public should also be made aware of it. It would be detrimental to our work for Swaraj to keep them in the dark. I have said that I still stand by the system of Government envisaged in *Hind Swaraj*."

The tragedy was that even Sardar Patel did not quite agree with Gandhiji's idealistic line. When Bapu was on his last fast, Lala Hansraj Gupta, Sanghachalak of Delhi, and many others went to Birla House to request him to give up his fast. Lalaji told me that Sardar Patel was sitting outside and he was muttering: "*Buddha na samajhta hai na marta hai*" (the old man does not understand and he does not die).

And yet in the India of 1947-48, Gandhi counted for more than Nehru and Patel combined. For he was simply the conscience of India.

While Nehru and Patel were thinking in politico-economic terms, Gandhiji was thinking in civilizational terms as explained in his *Hind Swaraj*. He was a real and total revolutionary. For him Man was more important than machine; full employment was more important than rapid industrialisation. He had a whole integrated philosophy of life. Had he lived even a little longer, he would have got English replaced by Hindi and other Indian languages; he would have got cow slaughter totally banned; he would have stopped the proselytising activities of missionaries and supported *Ghar Wapasi* (Back Home); he would have pressed with *Nai Talim*, giving children not just some bookish knowledge but also teaching them some art or craft for a living.

All this would have been very inconvenient for the British—and for Mr. Nehru, their choice for Prime Minister of India.

The death of Gandhiji removed the biggest corrective brake on Nehru. January 30 also weakened Sardar Patel vis-a-vis Nehru because the latter's friends now started saying tongue-in-cheek, that the Home Minister had failed to protect Bapu's life. (They would conveniently forget that Gandhiji had forbidden any search of persons attending his prayer meetings). Sardar's daughter, Maniben, writes in her 'Diary' that "Rafi Ahmed's intrigues against him, aided by Padmaja Naidu and Mridula Sarabhai, very much affected Patel's health. And Rajendra Prasad and Rajagopalachari both felt that Kidwai was endangering the country by creating a rift between Nehru and Patel. On Sept. 28, 1948, a police inspector awakened Nehru at midnight to inform him that a man was already on his way with a pistol and Rs.10,000 in cash to kill Sardar Patel" (Maniben's Diary, p. 17). Azad wanted Patel out of the Government. And Lady Mountbatten wanted him moved out as party President.

Later Nehru even tried to stop the veteran Rajendra Prasad from becoming the first President of India. And as soon as Sardar Patel died in 1950, he forced out Purushottam Das Tandon, the duly elected President of Congress, and appointed himself Party President.

From the death of Patel in 1950 till the India-China war in 1962, Nehru was the master of all he surveyed. He told Lady Mountbatten that her annual visits were "the pivot upon which everything else revolved". And when she died he sent the Indian warship *Trishul* to strew a wreath of marigolds on the waves where her ashes had been

consigned! (Akbar S. Ahmed, *Jinnah, Pakistan & Islamic Identity*, Routeledge, 1997.)

Nehru left us the Kashmir problem and the Tibet problem. Even Maulana Abul Kalam Azad and Rafi Ahmed Kidwai, who had earlier sided with Nehru against Patel, now realised that the Sardar would have been better for the country. Interestingly enough, while Patel was alive, Nehru used to consult Azad and Rajaji as centres of some political power. After Patel, Nehru ignored them completely.

D.K. Barua was not being very original when, during the Emergency, he pronounced: "India is Indira and Indira is India." Asaf Ali writes in his *Memoirs* (edited by G.N.S. Raghavan): "When somebody asked Jawaharlal at the time of Chiang Kai-Shek's visit, something about India, he was reported to have said: "I am India" (p. 316). After Independence, Nehru used to humorously describe himself as "the last Viceroy".

The British had had their way - all along the line. □

Dr. Syama Prasad Mookerji & The Unholy Trinity

"They have killed him" shouted the Srinagar Superintendent of Police when Dr. Syama Prasad Mookerji died in Abdullah's jail.

Pandit Premnath Dogra, President J&K Praja Parishad, said: "The facts as I know them, the information that has been reaching me from different sources, has convinced me that his was not a natural death. There is a mystery about it which can be resolved only by an impartial commission of inquiry."

In her letter to Pandit Nehru, Shrimati Jog Maya Devi, 82-year old mother of Dr. Mookerji said: "I hold the Kashmir Government responsible for the death of my son. I accuse your Government of complicity in the matter."

Even fourteen years later, in a discussion with a disciple on June 7, 1967, the Mother of Aurobindo Ashram said: "The difficulty is to find some one who knows Sri Aurobindo thoroughly, who is capable of receiving his inspirations directly and has at the same time a very strong character with a power—a contagious power—and a force that can arouse the inert masses. For years I have been looking for that man, without finding him. There was a man who would

have done ... He was assassinated in Kashmir. He is the one who came here when we wanted to have a conference for the opening of the University, he presided over it. A rather tall man and strong. I forget his name. But it was in Kashmir that he was assassinated (not officially, of course: he "fell ill")."

The Mother was referring to Dr. Mookerji.

It is exactly fifty years ago since Dr. Mookerji passed away in mysterious circumstances in Sheikh Abdullah's jail. The younger generations may not have even heard of him. But he was a titan. Though leading only the 3-member Jana Sangh in the first Lok Sabha, he soon emerged as virtual Leader of the Opposition. Only a few days before Dr. Mookerji passed away suddenly, *The Illustrated Weekly of India* carried the cover story: "After Nehru, who? Mookerji or JP?" along with photographs of both leaders.

Syama Prasad was the very worthy son of a very worthy father, Justice Asutosh of Calcutta High Court. Born on July 6, 1901, he became Vice-Chancellor, Calcutta University, at the very young age of 33 and made a big mark on it. Though a barrister, his heart was never in law; it was first in education, later in politics, and all the time in culture and public affairs. So much so that he wrote in his diary on Feb. 1, 1939: "I feel ever and ever more the need for a regular substantial income." And yet his limited means did not limit his expanding public life.

He was elected to the Bengal Council on Congress ticket. But when he found the Congress neglecting Hindu interests, he resigned his seat and resigned from the Congress. Later he fought for the University seat as an Independent and again won. As the Muslim League demand for partition assumed menacing proportions, Syama Prasad joined the Hindu Mahasabha. And he made that party a force in Bengal in the face of Congress and Communist opposition. In the Calcutta Corporation elections the Mahasabha won almost half the seats.

The Congress refusal to join hands with Fazl-ul-Huq to give Bengal a coalition Government in 1937, forced Huq to join the Muslim League. Later, when Huq was disillusioned with the League and found Jinnah "more arrogant than any Pharoah of Egypt", Syama Prasad gave him a helping hand and became his Finance Minister. The two of them developed so much mutual trust that Syama Prasad even used to take Huq to Mahasabha Executive meetings. However, the British Governor was in no mood to tolerate a Huq-Mookerji ministry. He punished Midnapore for taking active part in 'Quit India' movement, by refusing to send any relief after a devastating cyclone. The British 'Scorched Earth Policy'—to prevent possible Japanese advance in India—subsequently led to unprecedented famine. In sheer disgust Syama Prasad accused the Governor of acting as "a loyal and distinguished whip of the Muslim League Party itself" and resigned.

When Gandhiji came out of jail and thanked him for all he had done, Syama Prasad said no thanks were due for duty done. Gandhiji invited him to join the Congress but he politely declined and continued to lead the Hindu Mahasabha.

When the 1946 General elections were announced, Syama Prasad suggested that Congress should leave some seats to the Mahasabha so that Hindu interests could be protected. But Nehru in his *naivete* refused, saying Congress would defeat the Muslim League in Muslim Constituencies. (Perhaps Mr. Jinnah was not wrong when he said that Nehru was like Peter Pan, who never grew up.)

On the eve of Independence, Sarat Bose and Suhrawarly launched the idea of an "Independent United Bengal", separate from both, India and Pakistan. Syama Prasad smelt great danger. He said 'Independent Bengal' will trigger movements for 'Independent Madras', 'Independent Bombay', 'Independent everything'. He opposed the move and said if India was to be partitioned on religious lines, then Bengal and Punjab must also be partitioned on the same lines. He used to say, Congress had agreed to the partition of India; he had partitioned Pakistan itself!

When Independence came Congress under Gandhiji's influence had the good sense to give half the ministerships to non-Congressmen. (They included Mookerji, Ambedkar, Matthai, Neogi, Shanmukham Chetty, Baldev Singh, H.C. Bhabha.) As Industry and Commerce Minister, Syama Prasad gave the country Chittaranjan Loco Works and Sindri Fertiliser factory. When, however, he found Nehru wanting in protecting the life, limb and honour of one crore Hindus in East Pakistan, he resigned in protest and launched the Bharatiya Jana Sangh in 1951.

During the campaign for the General Election of 1951-52, Nehru threatened to crush Jana Sangh. Dr. Syama Prasad retorted: "We will crush this crushing mentality." Although BJS got only three seats, it polled enough votes to be recognized as a National Party. And by sheer dint of his courage, clarity and character, Syama Prasad became virtual Leader of the Opposition. His orations on Preventive Detection Bill and the situation in East Bengal are classics. And then came the Kashmir issue. Although the Sheikh's cabinet and his National Conference executive were both very much for India, he and his friend Afzal Beg started having second and third thoughts, once the valley was cleared of Pakistani raiders. Particularly after his long secret talks with Adlai Stevenson, recent US Democratic Presidential candidate in 1952, he began to toy with the idea of an independent Kashmir. Nehru noted the shift. When the PM visited Kashmir, there was no National Flag, no National Anthem! He returned to Delhi a bitter man and denounced "foreign interference" as responsible for the complication of the Kashmir issue.

Additionally, the Sheikh now started grossly discriminating against Hindus of Jammu. Nehru attributed this to the Sheikh's old communal background. When Nehru wrote to him asking why he had not implemented the Delhi Agreement, the Sheikh did not even care to reply. Nehru told Karan Singh that the Sheikh was even avoiding to meet him!

Intelligence Bureau Chief B.R. Mullik also noted in his *My Years with Nehru* (Allied): "I was surprised to find him (Sheikh) a completely changed man from the time I had first met him in September 1949. He received me coldly and then gave me a long lecture .... He would have probably liked the entire Dogra community (of Jammu) to migrate to India and make over their lands to persons of his choice." In this situation the J&K Praja Parishad, ideologically close to BJS, therefore, launched in 1953 a massive movement for the complete integration of J&K State with the rest of India. Its unanswerable slogan was:

"Ek Desh Mein Do Vidhan,
"Ek Desh Mein Do Nishan,
"Ek Desh Mein Do Pradhan,
"Nahin Chalenge, Nahin Chalenge"

(There cannot be two Constitutions, two flags and two Heads of State in one country.)

Even the veterans Jaya Prakash Narayan and Acharya Kripalani supported the Praja Parishad position.

The Sheikh Government shot down thirty-nine and arrested and detained three thousand demonstrators in Jammu. The BJS responded by supporting agitation in Delhi and Punjab.

Although Syama Prasad very much wanted to take

up the East Bengal issue, he decided to first tackle the Kashmir problem. After an exchange of half a dozen letters, Syama Prasad wanted to meet Nehru to settle differences amicably, but the latter did not respond. Under the Sheikh's influence Nehru even disregarded Rashtrapati Dr. Radhakrishnan's advice to meet Dr. Mookerji before the latter left for Jammu. Syama Prasad therefore decided to enter J&K State without a permit, which rules he challenged as anti-national. However, before he left Delhi on May 8, he wrote to the Defence Ministry asking what was the legal position of the permit system. But there was no response from the ministry. He also wired the Sheikh that he was coming to the State to study the situation, see him and work for a peaceful solution of the problem. Again there was no response.

Just before he entered J&K State, GOI could have arrested him for wanting to enter the State without permit. But they did not. They let him proceed on the Ravi Bridge. On May 11, at 4 p.m. at the centre of the Bridge he was arrested under the State's Public Safety Act. (Also arrested with him were Vaid Gurudutt, Delhi BJS President and Shri Tekchand, BJS party worker.) The reason was clear: if he had been stopped on this side, he could have moved the Supreme Court. He was, therefore, handed over to the Sheikh because the writ of Supreme Court did not run there at the time! Later, when a Delhi Court directed Kashmir to send Dr. Mookerji to Delhi for a pending judicial inquiry in the Capital, the Sheikh refused! What guarantee was there, he said, that Dr. Mookerji would be returned to his jail! Obviously he wanted to "teach a lesson" to Dr. Mookerji for challenging his separatist authority. Dr. Syama Prasad and party reached Udhampur at 10.30 p.m. Here they were served dinner in the Dak Bungalow. Syama Prasad said: "I am very tired" and he said he was in the habit of going to bed early. He, therefore, wanted to spend the night in Udhampur. But the authorities said there was no room available in the Dak Bungalow and he was scheduled to spend the night at Batote, which is the highest point in Pir Punjal mountain range. They reached Batote at 2 a.m.! And at 7.30 a.m. they again started out, reaching Kazikundh at 1 p.m. After lunch, they left for Srinagar, reaching the Central Jail at 3 p.m. After preliminary inquiries they were taken to a small private cottage in a desolate hill-side, eight miles from the city.

This cottage was a cold cage, with just one 10" × 12" room and two still smaller rooms. Dr. Mookerji occupied the first room and Gurudutt and Tekchand, the side-rooms. When Pandit Premnath Dogra arrived on June 19, he was put up in a tent! Many times Dr. Mookerji saw snakes moving about. In the only open space available, one could take only a 2-minute walk. Dr. Mookerji wanted permission to stir out. The IG Prisons and the Jail Superintendent said "no problem", but the policemen later said that there had to be written orders. These came only on June 16, when he was too ill to walk around. And Nehru described this snake-pit as a "fine villa"!

Here, Dr. Mookerji was so ill-provided for that, in his letters to his daughter in Delhi, he asked for books, Nescafe, a tin of biscuits, a tin of Ovaltine, a bottle of hair oil, a muffler, a writing pad!

(Incidentally, two months later when the Sheikh—and his friend Afzal Beg—landed up in jail, reports B.N. Mullik, "they were enjoying all the facilities in the special jail. Their families were paid handsome allowances, all the educational expenses of their sons in colleges and they lived like nawab's sons; prisoners got special diet in jail. Their rooms were fully furnished with air-coolers in summer, there was no restriction on interviews with relatives and friends.")

One of the books that Dr. Mookerji read in jail was *Raj Tarangini*, Kalhan's chronicle of the kings of Kashmir.

Within three days of his arrest, Dr. Syama Prasad complained of cold and pain in his right leg and he ran temperature. He lost appetite. But there was no doctor around. There was no call-bell even to call his servant Devi Prasad. And a phone was available only in the Water Works office—and that too only on working days, and during office hours. Dr. Ali Mohammed came to the quick conclusion that it was dry pleurisy and prescribed streptomycin. Syama Prasad told him that his family doctor had found that this antibiotic did not suit him. But Dr. Ali dismissed it as out-of-date advice. They knew better now, he said. Even the Head of State, Karan Singh, came to know of his illness only after his death!

Dr. Mookerji's son Anutosh tried for 15 days for permission to see his ailing father but it was not given. His brother-in-law who happened to be visiting Srinagar was also not allowed to see him. When his condition grew bad he asked his family to be informed but it was not done. When his Counsel, Barrister Trivedi, MP, came for consultations, the DM insisted on being present. Both, Mookerji and Trivedi refused. When on being refused permission to take instructions from Dr. Mookerji in private, Shri Trivedi was planning to return to New Delhi, a leading citizen of Srinagar called on him in his hotel room and pleaded with him not to go till he had got Dr. Mookerji released. He warned him that "Dr. Mookerji will be killed". (A Superintendent of Police called on Shri Trivedi the following day when all was over. He took out his pistol and cried aloud: "they have killed him. I will shoot them".)

Following morning when they were allowed to meet alone, Mookerji told Trivedi: *Mere Bhai, panch baje to chale jana tha*" (At 5 p.m. - yesterday - I was about to pass away).

On this occasion the DM delivered to Dr. Mookerji over a dozen letters which had obviously been held back for days and weeks!

The whole thing was a physical, medical and mental torture. The only relief came with the news that BJS had defeated Congress in the Ajmeri Gate, Delhi Assembly, by-election. The main issue in this contest was Kashmir. And Dr. Mookerji felt reassured that the people were very much with BJS on this issue.

But on June 22, at 5 a.m. Syama Prasad sent a jail warder to call Vaid Gurudutt. The latter found him perspiring, depressed and on the point of fainting. Dr. Ali Mohammed was informed, but he arrived only at 7.30. He decided to move Syama Prasad to Government Hospital, ten miles away, when the Army Hospital was close by. It took another four hours to take him in a taxi in a sitting position. Gurudutt and Tekchand were not allowed to go with him and be in the hospital. The Jail Superintendent said he could not arrange their food in the hospital!

In the hospital from 9 p.m. to 12.30 a.m. on that fateful night, Syama Prasad was all alone, with one nurse and a dozen armed policemen! There was no oxygen to administer. At 1 a.m. a doctor gave him an injection as a 'precautionary measure'. But the same doctor refused to come when the nurse frantically phoned him that his condition had worsened.

In this situation he repeatedly remembered his mother. Before 5 a.m. on June 23, Gurudutt was woken up and taken to the hospital. Dr. Mookerji was dead! The nurse said he had passed away at 2.30 a.m.

Dr. Mookerji's habeas corpus petition was expected to be taken up that day. It was expected that he would be released. The people would have celebrated the event. Was he given any injection to make it impossible for him to go

out and join the celebration, even if the court ordered his release? Nobody knows. Only an enquiry could have clarified that and many other matters. Now news of his death had shocked the people. Over five hundred persons had collected. His body was therefore quietly taken out from the back-door! When Barrister Trivedi arrived, they gave him Syama Prasad's suitcase, watch, specs and fountain pen. But his attaché case and diary were missing!

The All India Radio did not give the news in the morning. And the afternoon news dismissed it briefly towards the end. But it grandiloquently talked of his body being draped in an expensive Shahtoosh shawl, as though that could cover up the foul deed. While other ministers were there to see off the body, the Sheikh was not there. However when the snag which had delayed the take-off had been corrected, he walked in, looking unconcerned, with a big blooming flower in his button-hole.

Although BJS had requested the body to be first brought to Delhi and then flown to Kolkata, the Government refused.

The news stunned the country, and particularly Kolkata. The whole city closed down. The question on all lips was: Death—or murder? Every other hour, newspapers issued special editions, reported the slow progress of the flight. The plane was deliberately delayed, hoping the people would go home. But nobody moved. Kolkata did not sleep that night. The plane landed at last at 9.30 p.m. And it now took nine hours to cover the 14 miles to Dr. Mookerji's house. The following day it took four hours to Keortala Ghat, with five lacs joining the funeral procession.

The great Syama Prasad Mookerji was no more. But the question: "Dead or Murdered", did not go away. And it never will!

Dr. B.C. Roy, Chief Minister of West Bengal, sent a telegram to the Sheikh, wanting to know why he had not

been informed about Dr. Mookerji's illness when he had been the latter's family physician for years, and how the Kashmir Government had allowed this to happen. But the Sheikh kept a guilty silence.

The condolence meeting called by the Sheriff of Kolkata in the University Senate Hall, was attended by the Governor and Chief Minister also. But since the Governor and CM could not criticize the Kashmir Government publicly, they quietly left by the back-door. The meeting continued under the Chairmanship of *Ananda Bazar Patrika* editor Shri Chapala Kant Bhattacharya. The meeting demanded an inquiry into death and the restoration of the missing daily diary maintained by Dr. Syama Prasad.

Perhaps the most moving condolence came from Fazl-ul-Huq who said: "The loss of the only brother I had in this world has driven me mad with sorrow."

Dr. Ambedkar said: "It is quite true that Dr. Mookerji entered Kashmir without necessary permit. But it has been very difficult for me to understand how he could have been detained by Sheikh Abdullah merely on the ground of entry without permit. Sheikh Abdullah should have sent him back to India. Instead he clutched to legal power which seems to have been invoked without legal grounds, as a matter of excuse to keep him in custody to avoid embarrassment which he and his movement were causing to the Government of India."

And Dr. Jayakar, veteran liberal leader, former Privy Councillor, and now Vice-Chancellor, Pune University, closed his university for the day in salutation to the memory of the former VC of Calcutta University. And he said: "To die in a prison house, locked there by his countrymen's Swadeshi Government, by persons with whom he shared power as a colleague, is a fitting termination of a warring life. ... Let us hope that this incident will make the

Government of India realize, in their self-complacent enjoyment of the chits of American visitors, the deep enormity of their behaviour, which ignored all the canons of fairness and justice accepted by civilized governments."

And Poet-Parliamentarian Harindranath Chattopadhya sang:

"A giant has departed ... lo the sun
"Of a colossal intellect has set. ..."

Nehru in his letter of condolence to Dr. Mookerji's mother had said: "If I can be of any service to you, you will please not hesitate to inform me." Lady Mookerji took up his offer and said: "I, the mother of the great departed, demand that an absolutely impartial and open enquiry by independent and competent persons be held without delay." But Nehru was not as good as his word. He failed to institute any inquiry.

Sheikh Abdullah claims in his autobiography, *Aatish-e-Chinar*; "Pressure mounted for an enquiry into the circumstances leading to Dr. Mookerji's death. I asked the Centre to appoint a committee, but no one paid attention." The Sheikh even goes on to say that Nehru dismissed him and detained him a few weeks later, to divert public anger against him, and direct the same against Abdullah.

Any objective student would hold both of them responsible for their respective roles in the tragedy.

The biggest single problem arose from Pandit Nehru's confused mind. Just before Dr. Mookerji left for Kashmir, Nehru said: "We are there because people of Kashmir wanted us to be there or a majority of them. If they do not want us, out we come, whether accession is legally binding or is complete or incomplete." But two days later when thousands of Naga hillmen in Manipur quit his meeting, demanding Independence, Nehru was furious. He described their action as "foolish, dangerous, separatist and anti-India".

Dr. Mookerji asked Nehru to be clear and consistent. What was wrong in Manipur could not be right in Kashmir. "Let us declare unhesitatingly that no part of the Indian Union, including Kashmir, belongs to the local residents living therein. The entire land of India belongs to the people of India as such. If any sections do not desire to live in India, they can go wherever they like, but they have no right whatsoever to further partition the country, thereby imperilling its safety and integrity."

However, such clarity and consistency was beyond Nehru. And the Sheikh could see it. In *Aatish-e-Chinar,* he writes: "A confidant of Jawaharlal Nehru, the then head of the Intelligence Department, B.N. Mullick, confirms in his book *My Years with Nehru,* that Jawaharlal told him that he had every sympathy with the Jana Sangh and the Praja Parishad's demand for a complete merger of Kashmir with India but was worried that it would create a furore in the Security Council."

Dr. Mookerji was the victim of Pandit Nehru's and Sheikh Abdullah's confusions. In the current case, Nehruji could have prevented his entry into Kashmir—or even detained him—in which case Dr. Mookerji could have moved the court. And that would have highlighted the issue of the illegality and impropriety of the Permit System, and have it ended, which it was soon after any way. There was no point in letting him enter Kashmir and then have him falsely arrested there under Public Security Law.

Actually, during Dr. Mookerji's forty days in Abdullah's jail, Nehruji had spent five days in Srinagar. Later he said he had gone round, enquired after his health and was told it was "excellent" and that he saw the villa from outside and found it "fine". Should he not have visited the 'fine villa', greeted his former colleague and fellow MP, and told him that his protest against Permit System having

been registered, they could all go home and later sort out things?

But perhaps things were not that simple—for Nehru. According to Durga Das (*From Curzon to Nehru*), "there were only three effective spokesmen of the Opposition during the Nehru era. They were S.P. Mookerji, Kripalani and Lohia. And all three believed Nehru to be the source of all problems. But only Dr. Mookerji was a real leader since he spoke for the largest group which opposed Nehru's policies. In oratory and debating skill he excelled all others who have followed him." So Dr. Mookerji was the only serious challenge to Nehru. He had to go if Nehru was to have his way in all matters. And now he was gone—how exactly, nobody knows. Nehru and Abdullah's cold, casual and cruel treatment of Dr. Mookerji bordered on the criminal. And then there was Adlai Stevenson, who had poisoned Abdullah's mind.

The Unholy Trinity was complete!

□

Kashmir Princess

On April 11, 1955, something very serious happened. *Kashmir Princess*, Air India's Super Constellation, blew up while on way from Hong Kong to Bandung, Indonesia. Leaders of Afro-Asian movement—including Prime Minister Nehru of India, Prime Minister Chou En-lai of China, Gemal Nasser of Egypt and President Soekarno of Indonesia—were to attend the Bandung Conference; and Chou En-lai was scheduled to take this flight to Bandung. Fortunately, China sensed mischief and Chou En-lai quietly went to Bandung via Yangon and Singapore. (Years later—in 1968—Red Guard magazine *Hung Tien-Hsun* revealed that China had sensed sabotage. One wishes Beijing had communicated its suspicion to Delhi so that the flight could have been diverted or even cancelled, by way of abundant caution.) But eleven Chinese officers and journalists had boarded this plane and all of them—and all but three of the Indian crew—died in this explosion. It was an acute embarrassment for India; but, for China, it was a big shock. For the whole thing was nothing short of a blatant attempt on Chou En-lai's life. It was clear that some saboteur(s) had planted a time-bomb on *Kashmir Princess* when it halted at Kaitak airport of Hong Kong for re-fueling and routine check. Actually bits of explosive and

time device were found inside the star-board under-carriage wheel bay of the aircraft in the Indonesian waters, where the plane had fallen.

The British authorities in Hong Kong started investigating the matter. Anthony Eden, Prime Minister of Britain, assured India and China that the mystery would be unravelled, and the guilty brought to book. China insisted on India being associated with the investigation. And India deputed R.N. Kaw of Intelligence Bureau - who later became RAW Chief—for the purpose. Later IB Chief B.N. Mullik also went to Hong Kong and met Governor Grantham and the police top-brass. Both, Kaw and Mullik, felt that the Hong Kong police were doing their best. But China was not convinced; it knew better.

Investigations revealed that USA had made time-bombs available to KMT, the emigre Chinese of Taiwan, one of whose agents, Chou Chu, had planted the bomb in *Kashmir Princess*. After a few days Chou Chu had even boasted to his family and friends that he had received six lac Hong Kong dollars for the job.

On May 18, Chou Chu, and his accomplice, Wu, escaped from Hong Kong in CIA's own private airline, Civil Air Transport plane, as a stowaway, and reached Taipei, Taiwan, beyond the hands of India, China or UK. Mr. Mullik writes that Nehru was "very happy at the success of the investigation, though of course the culprits had escaped." The whole thing was reminiscent of the gag: "The operation was successful but the patient died." Eden was furious that the real culprits could not be brought to book and scrawled the single word 'BAD' on his brief.

The Chinese Deputy Director of Information, Ministry of Foreign Affairs, Mr. Hsiung Hsiang-hu, was certainly wrong to ask for the arrest and prosecution of hundreds of persons who had come in any contact with Chou Chu

in his daily life. And Chou En-lai was also wrong to suspect Mullik of being in Anglo-American pay. Mullik was a man of integrity; but he was being naive in trusting the Hong Kong authorities. (Fortunately Chou En-lai had the good grace subsequently to withdraw his allegation.) But the big question remained: *Kashmir Princess* blew up on April 11. Chou Chu escaped to Taiwan only on May 18, full five weeks later. Why was he and other employees of the Hong Kong Aircraft Engineering Company, who had serviced the plane, not taken into custody immediately after the explosion?

It would seem that while Hong Kong was administered by Britain, it was really ruled by USA. Believe it or not but there were as many as forty-two Vice-Consuls in the American Consulate in the island-city of Hong Kong. Obviously they were CIA men, engaged in spying and sabotage in a big way. At one stage Governor Grantham had taken a tough line on CIA. But he was "warned (by Americans) that they would make it 'hot for him' in London unless he relented, which he eventually did" (vide *The Hidden Hand* by Richard J. Aldrich, John Murray, p. 311).

Mr. Mullik finds fault with Hsiung Hsiang-hu, for not coming out of his 'fortress' to see either the Governor or the Police Chief or even him in his hotel room. But obviously Hsiung knew better. He was not exposing himself by way of abundant caution. People who had sabotaged *Kashmir Princess* in hopes of killing Chou En-lai would not have hesitated to kill Hsiung.

It would seem that Mr. Nehru did not realize the utter seriousness of the sabotage of an Indian plane which was to carry the Chinese Premier. It was an act of war. But he had advised Kaw to "avoid being made a party to the dispute between the Chinese and the British." (R.N. Kaw's *Vignettes of Nehru*, Nehru Centenary Volume, p. 302). Fact is that it was not an Indo-British dispute. It was a dispute between

India – and China – on the one side, and UK – and USA – on the other. But India shirked its responsibility. And when Chou En-lai withdrew the monetary allegation against Mullik, "The Prime Minister was happy at the discomfiture of the Chinese Prime Minister and Indira Gandhi also joined in the laughter and congratulated me for winning the duel against Chou En-lai"! Mr. Mullik adds: "The Prime Minister said that the Chinese were strange people, they saw the shadow of imperialism in everything." The blowing up of *Kashmir Princess* was not a shadow of imperialism; it was a ghastly case of imperialism.

Reports Kaw: "At my last meeting with Chou En-lai in Beijing, when we reviewed the progress of the investigation, he was categorical that the British Government of Hong Kong would drag on the case until December that year, and then close it." And since Nehru had advised him to treat it only as a dispute between the Chinese and the British, and not to involve India in the matter, Mr. Kaw told Chou En-lai that he 'could not support his opinion'." Writes Kaw: "Chou En-lai gave me a stern look and said somewhat menacingly, 'so you disagree with me. We shall see whom time proves right'. This was at 2 a.m. in the office of the Prime Minister of China. I must confess that a chill ran down my spine."

There was reason enough for Mr. Kaw to feel the chill in his bones. Thanks to the *Kashmir Princess* incident, 'Hindi-Chini Bhai Bhai' fast gave place to Hindi-China bye-bye, culminating in the India-China war of 1962.

One must give USA credit for not hiding its game of driving a big bloody wedge between India and China. US Secretary of State Kissinger told India's Foreign Secretary T.N. Kaul in 1971: "You know it would be silly for the US to favour a situation in which 800 million Chinese and 600 million Indians form a group. That would be a price that

under no circumstances we would pay" (P.N. Dhar: *Indira Gandhi, Emergency & Indian Democracy*, p. 171).

The *Kashmir Princess* affair was staged to sour India-China relations. And more affairs would be staged in the years to come.

□

Lal Bahadur Shastri— 'Neat As a snow drop'

Since Independence, India has passed through many trying times. Partition itself was a big trauma. Emergency (1975-77) was another. The simultaneous foreign-inspired waves of terrorism in Punjab, Kashmir and elsewhere were yet another. But perhaps our worst period was 1962-65 when we faced serious military challenges from China and Pakistan.

In 1947, India was militarily strong. Gen. Cariappa, our Chief of Army Staff, had said at the time that in the event of war with Pakistan, our first halt will be at Attock on the River Indus. Pakistan, he said, had a grand total of eight tanks at the time. This position was allowed to be grievously eroded year after year.

Soon after Independence, Gen. Lockhart, our Army Chief, saw Prime Minister Nehru with his Defence Policy Paper. That very day a shocked Lockhart told Maj. General A.A. Rudra: "The Prime Minister took one look at my paper and blew his top. 'Rubbish! Total rubbish!' he shouted. 'We don't need a defence plan. Our policy is *ahimsa*. We foresee no military threats. Scrap the Army. The police are good enough to meet our security needs'." (vide Gen. D.K. Palit's biography of Gen. Rudra.)

Though in 1949, militant communism had taken over China and in the early fifties, Pakistan had joined USA-sponsored military blocs in West Asia and South East Asia, India continued with its Kumbhakaran sleep, snoring peace and 'Panchsheel' from time to time.

Mr. Nehru appointed his kinsman, B.M. Kaul—with experience in house-building and Hindi dramatics, but no combat experience—as Chief of Staff. This gentleman flaunted his proximity to the PM's house and hoped to succeed Nehru one day. He instituted an inquiry against Gen. Manekshaw and launched a secret inquiry against Gen. Thimayya for treason. Defence Minister Menon conferred with junior officers over the head of their seniors. As Gen. Kumaramangalam noted later, Menon played havoc with Defence. "He believed that he could defeat the Chinese by a volley of words."

In the summer of 1962, while Indian and Chinese armies were facing each other, eye-ball to eye-ball, and China had warned that "the flames of war may break out any time", the PM, DM and FM went abroad; and Kaul himself went on a month-long holiday to Kashmir! On Oct. 13, 1962 while on his way to Colombo, Nehru said at Madras airport: "I have issued orders to throw them out (of Thagla Ridge)"! Within days he was preparing to abandon Assam!! No wonder the Report of the Inquiry by General Brooks Hunderson and Bhagat into the 1962 disaster was suppressed.

Any sensitive democratic leader would have owned up his responsibility and promptly resigned. But not Nehru. Later he suffered a crippling stroke, but he still would not give up office. He even stage managed the 'Kamaraj Plan' to send all important Cabinet Ministers and even important Chief Ministers out. He was obviously clearing the way

for his daughter. (Earlier he had made her Congress President.) After some time he did call back Lal Bahadur Shastri to assist him. But even this recompense was purely cosmetic. Writes Kuldip Nayar in his book, *Between the Lines*: "If Mr. Shastri nurtured the belief that his Ministership was a stepping stone to Prime Ministership, he was mistaken. As soon as Nehru recovered from his illness all important files and papers went direct to him and Shastri would come to know about them many days later through the courtesy of the indulgent Deputy Secretary or Joint Secretary. 'I am only a glorified clerk', he often said."

Mr. Shastri wanted to quit the Cabinet, but two considerations made him stay. "One, the Syndicate did not want him to give up the position of vantage he occupied as Cabinet Minister, even though he was No. 4 in rank. Two, by quitting, Mr. Shastri feared that the impression that Mr. Nehru had nominated him successor when he brought him back into the Government would weaken. He decided to wait."

Mr. Nayar goes on:

"Many people at that time said—and told him so—that Nehru's behaviour was influenced by Indira Gandhi's 'hostility' towards him. At first he would never encourage such talk but later he used to go out of the way to find out if that was true. And in due course he became convinced that he was not uppermost in Nehru's mind as his successor. There was somebody else.

"I ventured to ask Shastri at that time: Who do you think Nehru has in mind as his successor?

"His daughter," Mr. Shastri said, (*Unke dil me to sirf unki larki hai*) without even a second's delay, as if he had already pondered over the problem. "But it wouldn't be easy," he added.

Shastriji's sudden death made it easy.

Pakistan had been emboldened by American arms aid and Chinese support. Our poor performance in 1962 had given it an inflated idea of its own strength. Nehru's fixation of low procurement price for rice and wheat had reduced food production and made India dependent on USA's PL-480. Also the fact that India was now led not by a well known leader like Nehru but by a short-statured "dhoti-wearing" Lal Bahadur, made Pakistan think that it could have the better of India.

Bakshi Ghulam Mohammed had been the Sardar Patel of Kashmir. He was the man who had stabilized the situation in that border State after the dismissal and detention of Sheikh Abdullah. Nehru's acceptance of Bakshi's resignation also in the name of Kamaraj Plan, destabilised the Kashmir situation once again. It was in this situation that Pakistan gambled on the 1965 war.

Pakistan started with Operation Desert Hawk in Kutch, followed it up with Operation Gibraltar in Chhamb, and was poised to launch Operation Grand Slam to capture the Akhnoor bridge. Loss of that bridge would have cut off the only road link of J&K State to the rest of India. This information was received in India from two important sources in Pakistan. Shastri, therefore, decided to launch a diversionary march on Lahore on Sept. 1, 1965, to take the Pakistan pressure off Akhnoor. (Only one minister in the Cabinet opposed the move—on grounds of "world opinion".) This shocked Pakistan and Radio Lahore began broadcasting mourning music. Within hours Pakistan withdrew troops from Akhnoor to protect Lahore. J&K State had been saved.

On Sept. 26, Shastriji made a historic statement on Ramlila Maidan, Delhi:

"Sadar Ayub ne elan kiya tha ki woh Dilli tak chahal qadmi karte hue pahunch jaenge. Woh itne bare aadmi hain, laheem

shaheem hain. Maine socha ki unko Dilli tak paidal safar karne ki takleef kyon dee jai. Hameen Lahore ki taraf barh kar unka istiqbal karen. (President Ayub had declared he would soon walk through to Delhi. He is a great person, high and mighty of stature. I thought he should not undergo the travail of such a long walk. We should ourselves march towards Lahore to greet him.)

His slogan '*Jai Jawan Jai Kisan*' now resounded all over the country.

But as the war raged, the position on the ground was that though we had the bigger army, we had to post it on two fronts – Pakistan and China. We had 742 heavy tanks and Pakistan 924. Although we had more planes than Pakistan, our Vampires, Hunters and Mysteres were no match for Pakistan's Sabre Jets and Star Fighters. It was the little Gnats that fortunately tilted the air balance in our favour. (At first the designer of 'Gnat', W.E.W. Petter was not willing to sell that plane to India. Nehru and Menon's pro-communist positions had made him think "you chaps are communists". It was only Air Chief Marshal P.C. Lal's interest in cricket that convinced him that people who played cricket "could not possibly be communists." That is how we got the Gnat, the smart little fighter doing zig-zags in the sky.)

But, early in September 1965, Americans in India were heard saying that before long India will have to shift its capital from Delhi to Hyderabad or Bangalore. They were so sure of the superiority of their Patton tanks.

However, within three weeks, Pakistan had exhausted 90% of its ammo; ours was 50% intact. Our anti-tank missiles from Russia knocked out Patton tanks by the dozen. We even displayed a captured Patton tank in a Delhi square. And on October 2, 1965, Lal Bahadur cut a 'Patton Tank Cake' on his 61st birthday. USA not only lost face, it feared loss of arms trade and so we decided to soothe its ruffled feelings and withdrew the Patton tank on display. But it was now, in the words of Shastriji, "an awakened India".

The inherent strength of India and the timely bold initiative of Lal Bahadur on September 1, had saved the day for India. All this while China was making aggressive noises. And some people even feared a bigger war. But Shastriji kept his cool. And meanwhile India had captured Haji Pir Pass and eight other infiltration points along the old cease-fire line and we had the upper hand. Since we had no intention of annexing any Pakistani territory and Pakistan had been taught its lesson, when the powers urged cease-fire we agreed. According to Asghar Khan, former Chief of Pakistan Air Force, "Ayub Khan's legs were shaking" when he announced to the press his acceptance of cease-fire on September 24, 1965. He knew that Pakistan had been put in its place. And now pressure was put on India to have talks with Pakistan. These talks began in Tashkent under Russian auspices on January 4.

Pakistan, though beaten, had not changed its habits. Old habits die hard. Its propaganda was still aggressive. Ayub would not shake hands with Lal Bahadur. And Zulfikar Ali Bhutto used unprintable language. (In the words of the then British High Commissioner in Pakistan, Bhutto was "a man born to be hanged".)

Towards the end of the talks, Ayub Khan said: *"Kashmir ke mamle mein kuchh aisa kar deejiye ki main bhi apne mulk mein munh dikhane ke qabil rahoon"* (Please do something about the Kashmir problem so that I may be able to show my face in Pakistan.)

To this Shastriji responded with admirable clarity and firmness: *"Sadar Saheb, main bahut maafi chahta hoon ki main is mamle mein apki koi khidmat nahin kar sakta"*. (Mr. President I am sorry that in this matter I cannot oblige you.)

There is no charity in politics; and none at all in international relations. And so at the end of it all, the two sides signed the Tashkent Declaration on January 10. S.M. Yusuf, who soon after became Foreign Secretary of Pakistan, said in his book on Ayub Khan that Pakistan had "conceded the substance of a 'no war' agreement in Tashkent; the rest was 'a matter of words'." India had prevailed militarily and politically.

And then there was a bolt from the blue. In the early hours of January 11, Lal Bahadur lay dead.

I got the phone call from my friend and colleague in the *Organiser*, Kidarnath Sahani (former Governor of Goa). Although it was very early in the morning it was not possible to go back to sleep. I went to office early that day only to find two-three telegrams on my table urging a post-mortem of the body.

Now it is true enough that a person can die suddenly. It is also true that Lal Bahadur had a heart problem in 1959 and again in 1964. But it is also true that only two hours earlier his Secretary, C.P. Srivastava, "had not noticed any sign whatsoever in Shastriji's condition to cause even the slightest apprehension. Quite the contrary." The question, therefore, arose whether it was a natural death at all.

I promptly left for 10 Janpath where Lal Bahadur's body had been kept for public *darshan*. I could see big blue patches on his face. I felt like shouting that that was a clear case for post-mortem. But I am not exactly a brave man like Ram Manohar Lohia, who had denounced the League of Nations from the Gallery in Geneva. I was afraid that my loud suggestion could create a scene and even bring in the police. However, the doubt in my mind remained. I understand that Lal Bahadur's eldest son, Hari, had requested post-mortem but he was brushed aside.

Shri Srivastava discussed the matter with British

doctors Lain West and Spiro. The two doctors were of the opinion that "this blue colour is quite consistent with a death due to natural causes. But they also felt that the greater degree of blue discoloration was probably due to the fact that blood had not been drained from the body for embalming and an unconventional mixture had been used for the purpose since "the technique and materials used were the best that could be managed in Tashkent at that time". However. Dr. West also said: "Without a post-mortem examination and toxicological studies, it is impossible to say absolutely that no poison was administered".

And so the question remains whether Lal Bahadur's death was natural—or induced by poison.

To get back to the sequence of events: The Tashkent Declaration having been signed, Shastri was "literally beaming" at Premier Alexei Kosygin's reception on the evening of January 10. Evidently he took little or nothing at this reception. When he reached his villa he was asked what he would have for dinner. Shastriji first said he was not very hungry and then asked for a slice of bread, some *saag* (spinach) and fruits. The meal was prepared by Jan Mohammed, cook of TN Kaul, our Ambassador in Moscow. Around 11.30 his personal attendant, Ramnath, also brought some milk which he drank. After 12.30 a.m., Ramnath was told to go and sleep. But at 1.20 a.m., the PM appeared at the door of the staff bedroom and asked for the doctor. Dr. Chugh was woken up. As the staff led Shastriji back to his bedroom, he began to cough. He was finding it difficult to speak. He said again and again! *"Arey Baap" "Arey Ram"*. Dr. Chugh came running, felt his pulse and gave him an intra-muscular injection. At the same time the doctor said in deep anguish and despair: *"Babuji aap ne mujhe mouka nahin diya"* (Babuji, you did not give me a chance). Obviously Babuji was already dead. The doctor had injected a dead body. It was 1.32 a.m. January 11, 1966.

Many have wondered why there was no bed-side buzzer. When he felt bad, he got up, walked his room, climbed a few steps and walked the other room to reach his staff. This could have only worsened his condition. No oxygen was administered to him. Was it because there was no oxygen cylinder available ... or was it because he was already dead when Dr. Chugh, the very first doctor, arrived?

Many, many more questions have been raised. According to Jagdish Kodesia, Delhi Congress worker very close to Lal Bahadur, Kosygin who had hurried to the villa, repeatedly asked Dr. E.G. Yeremenko, the first Russian doctor to arrive, to revive Shastri's heart but she said "That would be possible only if death was due to heart failure". Obviously she felt the problem had not been heart but something else. It is significant that the death certificate prepared by Dr. Chugh carries the signatures of six Russian doctors who had definitely arrived after death, but not that of Dr. Yeremenko, who was the first Russian doctor to arrive. On the other hand three days later, Russia came up with another medical report which now included two more names, Yeremenko and Shamirzayev! Two medical reports of one death are unheard of in medical history. The first report says "it *can* be considered that death occurred because of an acute attack of infarktmio cardo". The second report says "it *may* be considered that death was caused by myocardial infraction". Does 'may' mean the same thing as 'can'?

More. The first report says Dr. Chugh's injection was a mixture of glucose, adrenalin and potassium chloride. The second report says it was glucose, adrenalin and calcium chloride! Also, why was he given intra-muscular injection and not an intravenous injection, for quicker absorption?

However, the most damaging testimony comes from

Smt. Lalita Shastri in her interview to the *Dharmayug* published on October 4, 1970. She thought that Shastriji had *not* died a natural death. In his critical condition "he repeatedly pointed to the flask. Thinking that he wanted water, people present there offered it to him. Shastriji did not take the water but once again he pointed in the same direction. She suspected that the water in the thermos flask had been poisoned." She wondered why the flask disappeared after that and it was never recovered. She also wondered why Shastriji's diary, which he always kept under his pillow, had also gone missing.

She said that Shastriji had told her many a time that when he was in his early twenties, a learned astrologer had told him that he would struggle much and rise much in his life and that he would be 'killed' in a foreign country. "After becoming PM also he couple of times referred to this incident and said that only that particular prediction now remained to be fulfilled."

She also said that the body had bloated and gone blue. The kurta could be removed only with great difficulty and the vest had actually to be cut. The family was kept away even while giving the ritual bath to the body. It was on their insistence, that they were at last let in. Lalitaji noticed a hole at the back of the neck from which blood was still oozing out. This hole was purportedly, made for embalming purposes. But she also found two incisions making a + (plus) sign on the abdomen. What was that? Had the Russians taken out some stomach content for testing? What were their findings we don't know.

It must not be forgotten that Indo-Pak relations were pure poison. So much so that on January 10, after the PM had spoken to his family, his personal staff member "Jagannath Sahai suggested to the PM that it might be a wise precaution to avoid over-flying Pakistan when

travelling from Kabul to New Delhi. He recalled how the Pakistanis had only recently shot down the civilian plane in which Balvantrai Mehta, Chief Minister of Gujarat, had lost his life. They might do something similar again. Shastriji responded: 'Not really. President Ayub is a good man. And now we have signed a peace agreement'."

The goodness of Shastriji's mind did not cancel out the poison in relations. It was therefore very wrong to put Mr. T.N. Kaul's cook, Jan Mohammed, in charge of Shastriji's kitchen in Tashkent. It was as foolish as having Sikhs in Indiraji's security—after all that had happened.

Matters were not improved by the mysterious presence of Kaul's Chinese girl-friend in Tashkent. Eye-brows were also raised over Jayanti Teja's recent stay with Kaul in Moscow. Teja's shipping company was under a cloud; he was known to be hostile to Shastriji and Teja's rich American wife had died in Rome in suspicious circumstances. Dr. Ram Manohar Lohia, after examining all the available data, had come to the conclusion that there were reasonable grounds to suspect 'foul play'.

In these circumstances, the post-mortem having been missed, there was a clear case for a judicial inquiry into the death of Lal Bahadur. And the demand came not only from T.N. Singh, Shastri's lifelong friend and former Chief Minister of UP, but veterans like Krishan Kant, A.B. Vajpayee and H.V. Kamath. Shri T.N. Singh said: "I am more than convinced that Shastri did not die a natural death." But all that the government did to meet public suspicions was to publish a White Paper on the subject full four years after the event. The dishonesty of the whole thing was clear from the fact that this White Paper was presented to the Parliament on the last day of the Winter Session of 1970—so that there could not be a proper debate on the subject. MPs in the two Houses roundly denounced the 'White

Paper' as a Black Paper and asked for a three-man judicial inquiry. *The Hindustan Times, The Statesman* and several other papers endorsed the demand. Even the American news magazine *Time* had wondered at the time whether Shastri had died a natural death.

Matters were compounded by the fact that Mrs. Gandhi was the beneficiary of Shastriji's death and she had always been known to be hostile to him.

In his goodness Shastriji had invited her to join the ministry. He had even offered her a protfolio of her choice; and she had picked Information & Broadcasting. And although she was the junior-most minister, he had placed her third in the Cabinet—next only to Home Minister Nanda and Finance Minister T.T. Krishnamachari—and well above veterans like Chavan, Chagla, C. Subramanian, Sanjiva Reddy and S.K. Patil. And for the Commonwealth Prime Ministers' Conference in London, he had deputed Indira Gandhi and TTK. But she continued to snipe at him. When the PM appealed to the people to 'Miss a Meal' every Tuesday to get over the food crisis, she made fun of it. When Tamil Nadu exploded over the Hindi issue in January 1965—at the instance of CIA—she flew to Madras to upstage Shastri, though the Official Languages Act of 1963 had already assured English as long as necessary.

When Srivastava brought to Shastriji's notice that Indira Gandhi was saying the PM did not consult her, the PM said she hardly ever spoke in the Cabinet. Moreover she had been told that she could always see him on a priority basis but she never did. She had nothing to say, nothing to communicate. It was not for nothing that Dr. Lohia, her old friend, had described her as *Goongi Gudia* (a dumb doll).

But her cold war against Shastri continued. Shastriji, therefore, went out of his way to send her a message on December 12, 1965, through Jagdish Kodesia and M.P.

Bhargava, to take things easy. "You can be Congress President and Prime Minister after the elections in 1967, as I would not like to be Prime Minister a second time."

Thoughtful men thought very highly of Shastriji. Chester Bowles, the best man USA ever sent as ambassador to India, said he divided Indian leaders into two groups: "One group I call the Adamses, and the other the Jacksonians. The Adamses are people educated in the UK or US, therefore very anxious to prove to the Indians that they are not pro-American or pro-West. They have one foot in Asia and one foot in Europe, charming, attractive and bright people, but they are not thoroughly Indian or deeply Indian. Now Lal Bahadur Shastri was a Jacksonian; his roots were in India. He had never been out of India until after he became Prime Minister. And there are a lot of those. I have much more faith in that type of person for the future." (vide Bowles interview to Lyndon B. Johnson Library on November 11, 1969).

And Frank Moraes, veteran editor, said: "Lal Bahadur was a reserved, reticent man, not given to imposing blanket ban or uttering absolute opinion, but if he knew anything, he knew his mind. He also sensed and understood to an unusual degree the thoughts and minds of his countrymen. He was essentially a *desi* product with no glittering tinsel pretensions, and yet with a mind and outlook attuned to progress in the best sense of the term, unencumbered either by orthodox rigidities or by extravagantly modern notions or proclivities. He had, in the best sense of that much abused phrase, an open mind." Nehru, on the other hand, said Frank, was, in his own words, "a queer mixture of East and West, out of place every where, at home nowhere."

Ambassador J.K. Galbraith said of Shastri: "There is more iron in his soul than appears on the surface. He listens to every point of view, he makes up his mind firmly, and

once he has made them, his decisions stick – He is the kind of man who is trusted." Indira, on the other hand, was like 'Tricky Dick' Nixon, smart but untrustworthy.

It is sad to note that the lady continued to snipe at Shastri even after his death. She told Ved Mehta: "Basically, he didn't have a modern mind. He was an orthodox Hindu and full of superstitions. You can't lead a country out of poverty with superstition. You need a modern, scientific outlook for that" (vide *Portrait of India*).

Shastriji's Secretary Srivastava's response to that insinuation was "Shastri – an orthodox Hindu? True, he did not smoke, he did not drink, he was uncompromisingly vegetarian, he insisted on wearing his native dhoti, kurta and Jodhpuri coat in all times and countries and he believed in the ancient values and culture of his country. But this is where his 'orthodoxy' ended. It would be entirely incorrect to suggest that Shastri had any religious prejudices or that he was ritualistic or superstitious or that he consulted astrologers. The truth is, as I know personally, he had no such attributes at all; secularism as well as great respect for all religions, were articles of his faith." As a Kayasth child, he began his education with 'Bismillah' (in the name of Allah) ceremony, and he was very well versed in Urdu poetry.

Interestingly enough, while Indira never matriculated, never went to college, Lal Bahadur had done a doctoral thesis on the philosophy of Dr. Bhagavandas, who became India's first 'Bharat Ratna'. He was not 'Shastri' because he was Brahmin like 'Panditji' – he was Kayasth, a 'Verma', like the Menons and Pillais of Kerala. 'Shastri' was the degree conferred on him at that great seat of national learning, Kashi Vidyapith for his scholarship.

Lal Bahadur had lived his eventful life without a blemish. In the words of poet-saint Kabir, "I have laid down

life as pure as I got it at my birth".

Das Kabir jatan se odhi,
Jyon ki tyon dhar deeni chadariya.

As Morarji Bhai correctly put it: *"Main to ek purush hoon. Lal Bahadur mahapurush hain"*. (I am just a person. Lal Bahadur is a truly great person.)

The *Observer* of London described him "neat as a snow drop".

While Lal Bahadur lived and died clean, his death in suspicious circumstances, Mrs. Gandhi's cold war against him and her refusal to institute a judicial inquiry into it, left a question mark on her.

□

Pt. Deendayal Upadhyaya

He was a rare gem in this land of gems, *bahuratna vasundhare.*

—Shri Guruji Golwalkar

He was a man of godly qualities.

—Acharya Kripalani

He was in the line of India's nation-builders like Tilak, Gandhi and Subhas.

—Nath Pai

He was *Ajatashatru* (a person who had no enemies).

—Prof. Hiren Mookerji

If I have two more colleagues like him, I will change the political face of India.

—Dr. Syama Prasad Mookerji

He converted the Jana Sangh from a regional party into a National Party.

—The Hindustan Times

He daily prayed to the Motherland: *Patavesha kayo twadarthe.*

(May this body be shed in your service.)

—Atal Bihari Vajpayee

And now he joins the ranks of Jesus, Lincoln, Gandhi and Martin Luther King.

—K.M. Munshi

Who was this "Angel on two legs"?

He was Deendayal Upadhyaya, President of Bharatiya Jana Sangh.

Panditji, as he was endearingly called, was born in a poor Brahmin family in 1917 at Mathura. He lost both his parents in his childhood and was brought up by his maternal uncle, a railway employee. A scholar of Sanskrit and Mathematics, he joined the RSS and, together with Bhaurao Deoras, he made the Sangh a mighty force in Uttar Pradesh.

BJS Founder President, Dr. Mookerji, appointed him General Secretary. Before long he emerged thinker, writer, orator, organizer, all rolled into one, a consummate leader. He read all the Five Year Plans. And he came out with original ideas on issue after issue. He said we must provide water for all fields, give work to all hands (*Har khet ko pani, har hath ko kaam*). Forests were important, but *vanavasis* (forest tribes) were not any the less important.

He said all Indian languages were national languages and recruitment tests for jobs should be through the mother tongue. Selected candidates can be subsequently required to acquire proficiency in Hindi and/or English. He wanted states reorganized into smaller units, as Janapadas. To the leftists who accused BJS of being "right reactionary", he said the concepts of 'Right' and 'Left' were alien and irrelevant to India. The BJS, he said, criticized USA for Indian national reasons; Communists criticized it only for Russian Communist reasons. The country could be developed and taken forward only through the strong and sacred appeal of nationalism. Indian Muslims were also 'Hindu', and 'Hindu' was not a religious term; it was a political term, covering all loyal citizens.

He said Swami Dayanand had made war on social untouchability; Jana Sangh would make war on political untouchability. He, therefore, blessed the SVD Governments, including all parties from BJS to CPI, in 1967. As a result you could go from Punjab to Bengal without setting foot on any Congress territory. The NDA Government, covering a host of parties, was a fruit of that integrated and inclusive thinking. He even developed the philosophy of Integral Humanism, emphasizing the unity and sanctity of all life.

The Calicut session of BJS in December 1967 was such a tremendous success, that *Matribhoomi*, the biggest Indian daily of the time, said it seemed the sacred Ganga had started flowing through Kerala. Deendayalji appeared like the Polar Star on the Indian political firmament. Evidently powerful mysterious forces did not fancy the emergence of a first rate nationalist on the Indian scene. Within six weeks of the Calicut session, on the morning of February 11, 1968, his body was found in the railway yard at Mughalsarai, UP.

The whole country was shocked and stunned into silence. From President Zakir Hussain down to Vice-President V.V. Giri, Prime Minister Indira Gandhi, Deputy Prime Minister Morarji Desai, veterans Jaya Prakash Narain and Acharya Kripalani, Speaker Sanjiva Reddy, Violet Alva, Fakhruddin, Humayun Kabir, Bakshi Ghulam Mohammed, DMK and Communist leaders, and ambassadors, called at BJS headquarters, 30 Rajendra Prasad Road, New Delhi, to pay their respects. All party flags flew half-mast in Delhi. On the evening of February 12, Panditji's mortal remains were consigned to the fire at Nigambodh Ghat.

It was clear as daylight that it was a case of political murder. But from day one, Government took the line that either it was an accident death, or killing by thieves, or simple murder, and not a political murder. Why the Government took this false and frivolous position—for what fears and/or under what compulsions—is not known. But the authorities clearly suffered from a guilty conscience. For, sixteen years later, John Lobo, the Deputy Inspector

General of Police, CBI, who had investigated this case, wrote a long 4-page article in the *Illustrated Weekly of India* (June 17, 1984) regurgitating the silly old story of thieves as murderers. The facts of the case, however, gave a lie direct to this theory.

Panditji boarded the Pathankot-Sealdah Express at Lucknow at 7 p.m., February 10, for Patna. The bogie was half first-class and half second-class. The first class half had three compartments – A,B,C, with 4, 2 and 4 berths respectively. Panditji's reservation was in A, whose other occupant was Shri M.P. Singh, Assistant Geologist, Government of India. The occupant of coupe B, Shri Gauri Shankar Rai, a Congress MLC, was requested to change places with Deendayalji, who liked to read late in the night, and he readily agreed. 'C' had one Major Sharma who never took that seat. At about 12.30 a.m., Kanhaiya, Secretary of BJS leader Raja of Jaunpur, met Panditji at Jaunpur Station and delivered him a letter.

The Sealdah Express goes to Calcutta *via* Gaya and does not touch Patna. The train reached Mughalsarai at 2.10 a.m. on platform No. 1. This bogie was detached, shunted and attached, on platform No. 2, to Delhi-Howrah Toofan, which left at 3.14 a.m. for Howrah *via* Patna.

Soon after 3.00 a.m. a line-man noticed a body lying straight, wrapped in a shawl, the head resting on a junction box, and a five rupee note prominently protruding from his right hand, and reported the matter to railway police. However, the body was brought to the platform only some six hours later. The fact that the deceased had a first class ticket and wore a wrist watch bearing the name of Nana Deshmukh, roused curiosity. A crowd collected. Some of them recognized Panditji. One of them, Vanamali Bhattacharya, ran to the city to inform Mughalsarai BJS people, who rang up Lucknow. Lucknow rang up Delhi, where the

BJS Parliamentary Party was meeting at 1, Feroze Shah Road.

At Mokameh, around 9.30 a.m., somebody found an unclaimed suitcase in compartment 'B' and handed it over to railway authorities. It was Panditji's suitcase.

Meanwhile at 6.00 a.m., Kailashpati Mishra, Bihar BJS Secretary, had gone to Patna Railway Station to receive Panditji. Not finding Panditji, or anybody else, in the Lucknow bogie, with all its doors wide open, Kailashji thought that perhaps he had gone to Delhi on Bhandariji's special request to attend the Parliamentary Party meeting there. He, therefore, did not look under the berth, where Panditji's suitcase was lying.

The official case was that two thieves, Ram Avadh and Lalta, had entered the compartment at Varanasi. They stole the *jhola* of Panditji who allegedly threatened to report them to the railway police at Mughalsarai. To this end, they said, Panditji went and stood at the exit, when the two thieves pushed him out of the running train. Panditji, they said, hit a pole—traction pole No. 1276—and fell down dead. When the train reached Mughalsarai, the thieves, they said rolled up Panditji's bed in a hold-all and walked away.

Witness after witness kept changing his testimony to fit the latest CBI theory. They said one thing to CID, another to CBI. The daily register of GRP was found over-written. The Judge inspected the register and found alterations and overwriting. Even John Lobo held them guilty of making "prevaricating statements about the exact time when they had first sighted the body."

Lalta had told the court that he had been kept in solitary confinement, tortured by the CBI at the Circuit House and daily beaten by Deputy Jailor Parasnath, to own the crime.

Ram Avadh told the court that the police offered him land, houses and Rs. 10,000 in cash for making the desired statement.

Asharafi Lal Mishra, Deputy Jailor, Varanasi, said both Lalta and Ram Avadh had been in the District Jail for theft but they had never been charged with anything more than theft, and never been charged together.

Both of them had been kept in solitary confinement for more than three months, against the rules. Under these circumstances, they had made forced confessions, which they repudiated in the Court.

Since there were no blood marks either in the compartment or on the pole—or on the ground where his body was found—it was clear that murder had taken place at a third spot.

Dr. Patankar, Additional Civil Surgeon, Varanasi, who conducted the post-mortem, said that Panditji had died of head injury - a 1.5" deep depression - though there were ten other injuries on the body, some of them by "dragging". The circular head injury could have been caused only by a hammer stroke and not by a pole hit. In any case two parallel impressions, each 5 cm in width but only 5 cm apart, could not have resulted from the traction pole, the steel channels of which are each 7.5 cm wide and more than 10 cm apart. The stomach and bladder were empty. The heart was completely devoid of blood.

Prof. Dr. K.P. Singh of BHU said that if someone were to fall from the train when it was going at a speed of 20 miles per hour, he could never strike against the pole because the descent from the gate to the ground would take about five seconds and the body could not be thrown very far.

Dr. N. Dass, ex-Director, State Forensic Scientific Laboratory, Calcutta, said that if the dead body had remained in the position in which it was found, the marks of the flow of blood on the clothes could **not** have been as they were found.

Dr. C.L. Garg, Director, Central Research Laboratory,

Hyderabad, who was in Mughalsarai from Feb 13-15, said that he had brought the door of the fateful bogie in front of the pole and swung his body fully by catching hold of the handle and found that a body could **not** strike the pole in that position. He was told to stop his investigations and go back to Hyderabad.

It is significant that there were three pointed steel brackets under the body as it was found, but there was not a scratch on the body at those points. And had the body fallen, the ballast would have been disturbed but, in this case, it was not.

Dr. R.N. Kataria, leading surgeon of Delhi, who examined the body in Delhi on the night of Feb 11-12, said that he found no blood anywhere near the leg fractures. This meant that death had occurred and the blood circulation had stopped when the fractures were caused. The blood stain on the sole of the deceased's shoes meant that the dead body had been brought from somewhere else and then deposited near the pole.

M.P. Singh deposed that between Varanasi and Mughalsarai, a distance of thirteen miles, he was awake and reading. Every time he looked into Cabin 'B', he did not see anybody inside, but he saw the bedding and file lying there. Where was Panditji? When the train was about to leave Mughalsarai, he saw a young man wearing dirty pajamas looking flustered. "I asked the man in the corridor what was the matter and he pointed to Cabin B and asked "Where is he?" I asked him "Who?" and he said: "My *Pitaji* was there". To this I said he must have got down. Thereupon this man ("he did not look like Deendayalji's son") went into Cabin B, picked up the file lying on the table, placed it on the bedding, which he rolled up hastily and carried it out. Till then this bogey had not been detached nor was any shunting going on.

Conductor B.D. Kamal said that he had checked tickets and found a person in civilian dress standing in an unlighted Cabin 'C'. Assuming him to be Major Sharma, in whose name the reservation stood, Kamal queried: "Major Saheb?" and this person said "Yes". Since Kamal's statement went counter to the prosecution line - Sharma had never taken this berth - he was dropped by the prosecution and was called only as court witness.

At Varanasi, Kamal came to wake up M.P. Singh. But Singh was already awake. Here a clean shaven person in pajama speaking in English told the conductor that the person 'Major Sharma', in Cabin 'C' that he had come to wake up, had already detrained. But according to Kamal, no Major Sharma had asked to be woken up. The Sessions Court viewed this mystery man "a nervous impostor who is pretending that everything is alright".

After going through all this evidence, the Special Sessions Judge, Shri Murli Dhar, came to the conclusion that prosecution had "totally failed" to prove the offence of murder against thieves. However, since Panditji's bedding items were reportedly found from different persons connected with them, they were found guilty of stealing under Section 379 I.P.C. and sentenced to four years in jail.

A top leader of the country had been murdered and his murderers had not been found. The whole country was scandalized. The cry went up for a judicial inquiry into the matter.

Even *Blitz* (June 14, 1969), sworn opponent of BJS, wrote: "We support the Jana Sangh's demand that Government should appoint a Commission of Enquiry to bring to light the HIDDEN TRUTH about the murder of Deendayal Upadhyaya.

"As Blitz's own investigations had pointed out, the assassination bore all the marks of a **political crime,** comparable to the Gandhi, Liaquat, Kennedys and King murders.

"Yet both the Central and State Police appear to have deliberately avoided investigating this angle in order to make it out to be a case of simple murder for robbery, and pin the crime on to obvious scapegoats."

The choice for inquiry fell on Justice Chandrachud of Bombay High Court.

Justice Chandrachud started off promisingly enough. He said: "If there is even a fraction of doubt about Panditji hitting the traction pole and dying, or his being thrown out and killed, then the Jana Sangh case (that it was a political murder) must be true." But within days he was echoing the CBI line that it was a case of thieving, leading, incidentally, "collaterally to death."

The Chandrachud Report, and the Report on Lal Bahadur Shastri's death in Tashkent, were presented to Parliament on the last day of the Winter Session of Parliament in 1970—so that there would be no opportunity for a full discussion on the subject. But Shri Vajpayee hammered the Government on the two issues and he had the entire opposition with him. His demand for a three-judge inquiry into Panditji's murder was endorsed by all opposition parties, including Dr. Ram Subhag Singh (Cong-O), Dnaneshwar Mishra (SSP), P.K. Deo (Swatantra), Prakash Vir Shastri (BKD), Randhir Singh (Cong-I) and even Jharkhande Rai (CPI). There was reason enough for the demand because Justice Chandrachud had done gross injustice to the case.

The critical questions that had arisen from the case were:

1. Where was Deendayal when the train reached Varanasi?
2. Who was the "nervous impostor" in front of compartment 'B' at Varanasi?

3. How did the Rs. 5 note come to be put in Deendayalji's hand?
4. Why would a 'murderer' come back to the compartment - since he could be caught - just to pick up the hold-all, and not even look for the suitcase?
5. How can a man thrown out of a running train and hitting a pole, fall straight down like a stick with the note still in his hand, the shawl still nicely wrapped around and the head squarely resting on a junction-box as if it were a pillow?

The good Justice Chandrachud "arrived at the conclusion that Shri Upadhyaya was pushed out of the train, as a result of which he dashed against the traction pole" and died.

And he responded to the above questions to fit his 'conclusion'. He assumed that he had been pushed out, although M.P. Singh, the only other passenger in the bogie, wide awake for the thirteen miles of Varanasi-Mughalsarai, did not see anybody—either Deendayal or any thief. Even the 'thief' appeared only when the train was about to leave Mughalsarai. Since M.P. Singh's evidence disproved the CBI theory, his father, Ram Swarup Singh of Moradabad received two anonymous letters threatening his son's life. The father therefore made some security arrangements for his son.

Nor did he explain why there was not even a drop of blood on the pole - or on the ground where he had allegedly fallen.

He said Panditji had probably taken out the Rs. 5 note to send a telegram to Patna that he was coming. Panditji did not need to send any telegram because Patna knew he was coming. And if at all such a telegram was needed,

Lucknow would have sent it. Even assuming Panditji wanted to send a telegram, where is the message? Surely money would not be taken out before the message was passed on. Also it is significant that the note was lightly held and could be easily removed. Had the note been there when Panditji was killed, the *rigor mortis* would have made it difficult to take it out.

He explained away some blood stains on the pillowcase as possibly due to 'bed-bugs'!

On page 84 of his Report he said: "The question whether Shri Upadhyaya was alive at Varanasi shall have to be dealt with independently on a separate footing," but he failed to deal with it anywhere in his report. Here was Operation White-Wash in excelsis.

One hopes it was not for services rendered in the Deendayal Murder Inquiry that he came to be appointed Chief Justice of India. And one hopes it is only a coincidence that his son has been appointed High Court Judge at a very young age and he can be expected to become Chief Justice of India for several years.

Shri Harish Chandra, Lucknow BJS Secretary, Shri J.T. Wadhwani, Bombay BJS Secretary and Shri Vasant Bhagwat, Maharashtra Organising Secretary, said that when they went to see off Panditji at Lucknow and Mumbai respectively, after the Calicut Session, they found a stranger in both cases, inexplicably hovering around. They did not realize it at the time but now they felt that Panditji was probably being shadowed by a killer group.

When the Deendayal murder took place, the Jana Sangh in its innocence, asked for CBI inquiry in the expectation that it would be better equipped to unravel the mystery. But within days a retired IPS officer the party had informally associated with the inquiry, came and told Shri Krishanlal Sharma in my presence that Government did **not** want to

find out the truth. He said that whenever any information was received about who was saying what and/or doing what, CBI would call the persons named, ask them if the report was true. The latter would deny it and that was the end of the matter. The CBI never asked Ram Avadh who had told him to go and get that bedding.

Since there was not a drop of blood either in the compartment or at the spot where the body was found, it is clear the killing took place elsewhere. It would seem that Panditji was administered chloroform to make him unconscious and then taken down at one of the wayside stations.

Shri Ramashankar Singh, a draftsman in the Government Irrigation Department, Lucknow, told the Chandrachud Commission that a couple of minutes after the train left Jafarabad, he first heard a shriek and then a thud—"third class sounds from first class compartment". Shri Ramesh Chandra, an acquaintance travelling in the same compartment, also heard it.

Incidentally, the editor *Organiser* got two-three phone calls soon after Feb 11, 1968 saying Panditji had been pulled out of his compartment, taken away and killed. Since, however, the calls were anonymous, he could do nothing about it. Only the CBI could have followed such clues but it would not!

This Operation Abduction could have been done by one or more persons entering the bogie at Shahganj, Jaunpur or Jafarabad. When Shri Gauri Shankar Rai detrained at Shahganj, only M.P. Singh and Deendayal were there as bonafide passengers in their respective compartments.

In an unconscious condition Panditji seems to have been given the fatal hammer stroke on his head. Later he was hit by an iron rod on the back and his legs broken. Just before the body was sighted in the Mughalsarai Yard,

a car was reportedly found standing on the track in the railway crossing very close by. This car seems to have been used to transport the body to Mughalsarai. No effort was made to trace the car and interrogate persons working close by. The local press reported that a sum of Rs. 400 had been given to some employees to delay the shunting, for more time to place the body where it was found; but again the matter was not probed.

Nana Deshmukh informed the CBI that at 4 a.m. on that fateful night when Prabhu Dayal, fitter, went to S.N. Tiwari, Train Examiner of Akbarpur, for keys etc., the latter told him excitedly that Jana Sangh's Deendayal had been murdered. Prabhu Dayal's written statement was handed over to CBI. The CBI just asked Tiwari if that was a fact and when he denied it, it just closed the matter!

Twelve persons belonging to a particular group were found missing from their place of residence and gathered in Mughalsarai. Once again the CBI did not investigate the matter.

A section of the Press (including *Blitz*, Mir Mushtaq Ahmed's *Asia* and Jamati Islami's *Radiance*) attributed the killing to extremists and even named Balraj Madhok. Vajpayee dismissed the insinuation as obscene.

More. The actual Major Sharma of course never came there. But according to M.P. Singh and Gauri Shankar Rai, a man with huge whiskers was seen in Cabin 'C'. They thought he was 'Major Sharma' but, they said, this man did not look like a Major at all. "Though he was dressed in khaki he wore no signs of rank (vide *Organiser*, Feb. 25, 1968). Who was he?

Well, here Kailashpati Mishra has something to say. Senior RSS workers of Buxar had told him that a Brahmin of Pathakpura had gone to Kashi for the treatment of his daughter. Since the train stop was brief he tried to enter

the first class compartment in which Deendayalji was travelling, but a hefty Pathan pushed him back. He recognized this Pathan as a muscleman of Bara village, District Ghazipur. Before this poor Brahmin could get up, the train left. Later when he learnt of Panditji's death he put two and two together and told this Pathan in Bara: "You killed a Brahmin." The Pathan simply laughed. RSS workers rushed to Bara to locate the man but by then he had left for Nepal where he was reported to have been murdered. Was he murdered to ensure his silence? (vide *Manthan*, July-Sept, 2000).

Perhaps the most sinister part of it all was the receipt of scores of letters from 'Tippu Sena' **written in the same hand but posted from different places in the country,** threatening 'Mughalsarai' to RSS and BJS leaders. Letters also went to the editor *Organiser* and veteran journalist Syed Jeelany, a regular columnist of *Organiser*. Nana Deshmukh produced sixteen such letters in the court.

Dr. Jeelany wrote the article 'Who killed Deendayalji?' (*Organiser*, August 24, 1968) in which he mentioned that he had been threatened with Mughalsarai by "Tippu Sena, Farj Mohalla, 10/68 Dakkar Street, Bangalore-2". Inquiries in Bangalore revealed that there was such a locality and there was an Urdu paper in that area, but the premises mentioned in the address did not exist. Dr. Jeelany added: "A few days afterwards I received from the same quarter, a communication in the name of a memorandum which asked me to act as a 'mediator' by approaching the leaders of the RSS and Jana Sangh to work out an equitable solution of the communal problem." The memorandum bore the same address in Bangalore and was in the same handwriting. It mentioned Mr. A.G. Noorani as a confidant of my correspondents and asked me to work in cooperation with him. "I did not like this at all. Mr. Noorani was known to me only by hearsay as an Indian Muslim of the second generation and a barrister who writes on political affairs. I had read many writings of his which gave me the impression that he was possibly a publicist in Pakistan's pay or an exponent of the CIA's Grand Strategy."

Yet another letter received by Dr. Jeelany was written in the self same hand but it was this time post-marked Salem (Tamil Nadu).

Here were these threatening letters written in the same hand but posted from different places. What was this mysterious Central Incendiary Agency, threatening murder to RSS-BJS leaders? The CBI did not probe this sinister matter.

Government just was not interested in honestly investigating Deendayal's murder, for fear that it might lead to inconvenient findings, compromising Government's relations with forces internal and/or external.

It is significant that notwithstanding repeated requests Government did not announce any award for information leading to the unravelling of the mystery.

The murder of Deendayal will remain a mystery until and unless the secret files of the Government of India and, may be, of some foreign powers are made public.

□

Mrs. Indira Gandhi

I have never been enamoured of the Nehru family. But I can never overlook or condone the murder of Indira Gandhi. The murder of a Prime Minister is something much more than the killing of an individual, however important, it is an assault on, and a challenge to, the country.

Stanley Wolpert is very right when he says: "When the tanks rolled into the Golden Temple (Mrs. Gandhi) had signed her death warrant." But why did she do it? The explanation lies partly in the character of Mrs. Gandhi, and partly in the nature of the Punjab problem, but more than both these it lies in the incitement and abetment of violence in India by foreign forces.

First the persona of Mrs. Gandhi.

No less a person than Bishan Narain Tandon, Joint Secretary in the Prime Minister's Office in the crucial years, 1969-76, says of her (vide *PMO Diary*, Konark) that she "did not hesitate to lie" (p. 111) and that in her corruption, "even Nixon will be put to shame" (p. 371). Although she went butterflying from Allahabad to Shantiniketan to Pune and Geneva, she never matriculated and she never saw the inside of a college. In the lack of formal education "the PM's mind is very disorganized." He adds: "I have always held that three qualities are needed to lead this country: character,

character in its broadest sense, ability and tolerance. Unfortunately the PM is deficient in all three." Her Press Secretary, Sharda Prasad, noted that the PM operated on "advice tendered at the lowest level" *viz.* her P.A. Mr. R.K. Dhawan, "on things about which he knows nothing." (p. 40). Her right-hand man P.N. Haksar moaned that "I was forced to go to every judge in connection with her election case" (xlvii).

She didn't trust anybody—and nobody trusted her. When on her first election as Leader Congress Parliamentary Party—which made her Prime Minister - she went home to No. 1 Safdarjang Road, there was no near or dear one to greet her or felicitate her.

She would shout and scream and threaten to resign over trivial issues, in the presence of many persons. Her Principal Secretary, P.N. Dhar, aptly described her tantrums as "her Kathakali dance" (p. 77). Tandon found her "a very difficult person, outwardly civilized and decent but totally lacking in cordiality" (p. 127).

Second, the Punjab problem. Here was a frontier region that had borne the brunt of a thousand years of foreign invasions. Historically, it was the Sikhs who retrieved the Punjab situation for India. Shri Guruji Golwalkar, Sar-Sanghachalak RSS, aptly described the ten Sikh Gurus as "super-human". The Sikh community became the Forward Bloc of Hindu or Indian Society. When Nadir Shah and Ahmed Shah Abdali looted India, it was the Sikhs who, with their guerrilla tactics, *Dhai Phut* (Hit and Run), looted the looters and retained Indian wealth in India. After Attock on the Indus was lost by Raja Jaipal to Mahmud Ghazni in 1002, it was the Sikhs who again hoisted the Kesaria Flag on Attock Fort in 1813. But for the Sikh resistance - and renaissance - India would have lost much more territory to Pakistan in the event of partition. After the Third Battle

of Panipat, Sikhs saved 2000 Hindu women taken captive by Abdali. The British occupied Hansi, now in Haryana, to prevent Sikhs and Marathas from joining hands. On Diwali Day, 1761, Ranjit Singh entered Lahore. In his humility he called himself just 'Singh Saheb' and not Maharaja. Punjab was now ruled by Punjabis, without distinction of caste or creed.

Dhyan Singh Dogra was appointed Prime Minister, Azizuddin Foreign Minister and Pandit Dinanath, Finance Minister. The Sikh commanders and landlords competed in protecting Brahmins and cows.

Ranjit Singh had lost one eye to smallpox in his childhood. In 1831, Lord Bentinck asked Azizuddin in Shimla, Ranjit Singh was blind in which eye. And the shrewd diplomat replied: "The spendour of his face is such that I have never been able to look close enough to discover that." That was the respect he commanded.

With the British power spreading all over India, and with Ranjit Singh gone, nothing could stop British take-over of the Punjab in 1849. Soon after came 1857. To begin with, the Sikhs were evenly divided between pro-British and anti-British elements. But the Sikh Princes' assessment that the British would win, swayed them to their side. And now began the British game of divide and rule along caste and community lines. Jats, Rajputs and Scheduled Castes, of whatever community, were declared martial races. And they were declared agriculturists, who alone could now buy agricultural land. In 1899, Kahan Singh, British-inspired Prime Minister of Nabha, produced the pamphlet, *Hum Hindu Nahin Hain.* The exasperated Maharaja said: "If we are not Hindus then whom shall we marry?" (Hindus and Sikhs have always freely intermarried.) Interestingly enough, even the Privy Council decided in 1903 that Sikhs were Hindus.

Guru Nanak Dev was born on April 15, 1469. But since this fell very close to Baisakhi on April 13, when Sikhs who visited Dera Baba Nanak, enthusiastically visited the adjoining Hindu temple, they got his birthday changed to November, courtesy the Singh Sabha toadies. And Swami Dayanand of the Arya Samaj did not help matters when, in his Vedic enthusiasm, he ran down Rama and Krishna, Mohammed and Guru Nanak.

But before long patriotism asserted itself. Ranjit Singh's minor son, Dalip Singh, who had been taken to London and converted to Christianity, came back to the fold, had *prayashchit* and *Ganga-snan*, and declared himself an "implacable foe of the British people." Namdharis - also known as 'Kukas', for their *kooks* or shrieks - wore khaddar and saved cows from slaughter even at the cost of their own lives. Sixty-six of them were blown from cannon-mouths. Many Sikhs — 376 — hired a Japanese ship, *Komagata Maru*, went to Canada as Commonwealth Citizens, were not allowed to land, were brought to Kolkata where 18 of them were shot dead. During World War I Sikhs joined the Gadar (Revolt) movement in USA in large numbers. When USA entered the war on the British side, they were crushed.

Before long the Sikh society stood divided between Singh Sabha conservatives consisting of loyalists, and Akalis. Singh Sabha was pro-British but it had traditional peaceful relations with Hindus and Muslims. The Akalis were anti-British. But since they were told by the British that they were not Hindus, they removed the idols and paintings of gods and goddesses which until then had adorned the Gurudwaras. Sikh-Muslim relations, of course, had never been great.

Provincial autonomy after 1937 gave Punjab a stable Unionist Government of Hindu, Sikh and Muslim land-

owners. Sir Sikandar Hayat, the outstanding Prime Minister of Punjab, rejected partition on religious lines. He used to describe the demand for Pakistan as 'Jinnistan', a double pun on 'Jinnah' and 'Jinn' (ghost). He also found the Sikhs 'insatiable'. But he died in 1942 and the Britishers pushed for Partition. Everybody - Hindus and Muslims - suffered; but Sikhs suffered the most. The Radcliffe Line put one-half of them in India and the other half in Pakistan. Master Tara Singh unsheathed his sword in Lahore. Muslim League leader Nawab Mamdot Khan gave the call for *Maro te Saro* (Kill and Burn). Amrita Pritam, the distinguished Punjab poetess wrote in agony: "When one daughter of Punjab cried (in Warris Shah's poetry) all Punjab cried; today lacs of Punjab's daughters are crying, but to whom shall they go now? (*Ik roee dhi Punjab di, tu lakh lakh maaree vain; hun lakhan dhiyan rondi hain, kis Warris Shah nu kahn?*) It was a titanic tragedy for all concerned.

Things nevertheless, began to settle down, but then the Arya Samaj made a Himalayan mistake. In the Punjab University Senate, Bhai Jodh Singh, Principal Khalsa College, Amritsar, and Principal Niranjan Singh, leading academician, long-time Congressman and brother of Akali leader Master Tara Singh, proposed that Punjabi in two scripts—Gurumukhi and Devnagri—be accepted as the language of instruction and examination up to matriculation. But the Arya Samaj friends, who dominated the Senate, in their excess of love for Hindi, refused. Shri Guruji Golwalkar was the only leader who urged Punjabi Hindus to accept Punjabi, their own language, with good grace, but to no avail. This soured Hindu-Sikh relations.

The Sikh thinking now was: Hindus got Hindustan, and Muslims got Pakistan, but they got nothing. This was not exactly correct. Hindustan or India belongs to all Indians—Hindu, Muslim, Sikh. And thanks to Sikh

enterprise, the per capita income in Punjab is almost double the national average. And full 25% of Sikh population lives outside Punjab. And they are doing very well. However, their grievance was that even after linguistic reorganization of States, a Punjabi-speaking State had not been carved out of bi-lingual Punjab. Fortunately that was also done in 1966 and 'East Punjab' was split into Punjab and Haryana. But now the Sikh brethren were on the horns of a dilemma: if all Punjabi-speaking areas were put together, the State won't have Sikh majority. And they thought Sikh identity will be secure only in a Sikh-majority State. So they left Punjabi-speaking Ambala District etc. out. In the process they lost much of industry, which was in Haryana, and much of forest land, which was in Kangra, now in Himachal Pradesh. But otherwise they were happy enough in their 'Punjabi Suba'. Some called it 'Subi' (a mini-State). However, the Congress under Mrs. Gandhi would not let Punjab in peace.

When the present Punjab State came into existence on November 1, 1966, the first Chief Minister was Giani Gurusnath Singh Mussafir of the Congress. In the 1967 General Election, Akali Dal formed a coalition government with BJS and Communists. But within months Congress organized a split in the Akali Dal and replaced Justice Gurnam Singh's Akali Government with Lachhman Singh Gill's puppet Congress Government. Gill used to boast: "It will be either Gill or nil."

In the 1969 mid-term poll, Akali Dal and BJS won an absolute majority. Prakash Singh Badal became Chief Minister. But within two years this government was dismissed by the Congress Centre. In 1972 Congress staged a come back. However, in 1977 Akali Dal and Janata Party (basically BJS) won a majority. But in 1980 this Government again was dismissed. (Before a Constitution amendment passed by the Janata Government in 1978, the Centre could dismiss a State

Government without seeking even Parliamentary vote on the subject. And so Punjab was on the boil.)

Before 1967, Akali Dal used to join hands with Congress. But under such an arrangement, Congress was the major partner and Akali Dal, a minor one. The Sikhs preferred alliance with BJS (later BJP) because in such an alliance Akali Dal was the major partner. This meant Hindu-Sikh camaraderie and peace in the Punjab. But this did not suit the Congress, which had an itch for monopoly of power. Zail Singh used to moan that "these people are not only in power they are actually popular".

Minor Congress Hindu leaders would tell 'Hindu' papers that it was 'Sikha-Shahi' in Punjab. Another set of Congress leaders - this time Sikh - would tell some 'Sikh' editors that under 'Jana Sanghi' Hindi influence, nothing was being done for 'Punjabiat'. Soon the fat would be in the fire. And then the Congress money—and Congress control at the Centre—would go to work and divide or dismiss a popular Akali-BJP (Sikh-Hindu) coalition. Mrs. Gandhi never realized that in monkeying with a border State like the Punjab she was playing with fire.

Akali politicians in their competitive politics, no doubt talked of fifteen—and even forty-five—demands. But they had never talked of 'Khalistan'—though that is the impression the Congress propaganda gave. It was the Sikhs in UK and USA, in league with their secret agencies, who had asked for 'Khalistan'. The capital of this 'Khalistan' was London - and never Amritsar.

The Akalis had perfectly peaceful and legitimate demands. Chief of these was transfer of Chandigarh, now a Union Territory with both, Punjab and Haryana Secretariats. However, they knew that under the terms of State reorganization, they could get it only by parting with the big market towns of Fazilka and Abohar, and they are not keen on that. Their second major demand is water. One can understand that in view of the fact that during the Emergency, Mrs. Gandhi had violated the expert award and given extra water to her lackey, Bansilal of Haryana. Their one and only real demand is that as and when they win an election they should be allowed to form their government and run it for the full term. No democrat can quarrel with that. But Mrs. Gandhi did just that.

At one stage she proposed to Akali Dal the Congress-DMK pattern of party alliance: the Congress to contest the bulk of Lok Sabha seats and the Akali Dal, the bulk of Vidhan Sabha seats. Badal went straight to his BJP friends for consultation. Mrs. Gandhi was furious. She is reported to have said: "Why should I give them anything, since they will again tie up with BJP in any case?" She did not realize that in a democracy, it is the people's will that will, and must, prevail. Indian democracy was not a gift of New Delhi. And she was not a Queen Empress who could confer or withhold 'gifts'. Democracy was the right of the people and not Centre's charity to the States.

The following day some Sikhs were got killed in Congress-ruled Haryana in a 'command performance'. That was the end of Congress-Akali talks and the start of mayhem in Punjab. In these troubled waters foreign-inspired terrorists went to work with a vengeance.

Congress now invented one 'Sant Bhindranwale'. His very first press conference in a Chandigarh hotel was paid for by Zail Singh, whom Mrs. Gandhi later made President of India. This 'Sant' now began to attack Hindus and make extravagant demands on behalf of Sikhs. The idea was to queer the pitch for Akalis and divide the Sikhs.

In 1981, Lala Jagat Narain, former minister, and editor *Hind Samachar* (Urdu) and *Punjab Kesari* (Hindi) was shot dead. The Congress 'Sant' blessed the killers. This was

followed by the murder of Romesh Chandra, Jagat Narain's son. Dr. V.N. Tiwari, M.P., BJP leaders Harbanslal and Babu, Principal R.N. Sharma of Ferozepur met the same fate. And every other day there were reports of beef being thrown into temples and Hindu bus passengers being separated and killed. No proper Sikh would do any such thing. And a whole lot of Sikhs were also being killed as 'police informers'. In April 1984, there were simultaneous attacks on thirty-nine local railway stations. There were even reports of Government agents doing some of these things.

Julio Ribeiro, former Police Chief of Punjab, writes in his autobiography, *Bullet for Bullet*: "In Punjab there were some persons with criminal propensities, who were known to police officers at various levels. They were approached and a few of them agreed to form groups which would move in the guise of terrorists. The police did give them financial and logistical support. (They) began to prey on law-abiding rich citizens." It was a mad, bad Government-terrorist competition in crime and violence.

Meanwhile in their obsession with security for Asian Games in 1982, the Haryana Police stopped and searched even retired Sikh Major-Generals like Jaswant Singh Bhullar and Narinder Singh. This scandalized the Sikhs.

Two things were specially mystifying. Bhindranwale was going far and wide, carrying on his raging, tearing campaign with armed terrorists by his side, but Government did not touch him. Tapes of his violent speeches were being played in some Regimental Gurudwaras, but again no action was taken. S.S. Mann as SSP Faridkot had been very close to Bhindranwale. He had even invited him to address police parades. He deserved to be sacked but he was not touched. Incidentally, he is *saandu* of Amarinder Singh, now Congress CM of Punjab. (Mann and Amarinder are married to two sisters.)

Earlier, on April 25, 1983, Sardar A.S. Atwal, Deputy Inspector General of Police, Jalandhar Range, was shot down as he came out of the Golden Temple, Amritsar. Punjab Chief Minister Darbara Singh, a life-long Congressman, wanted to send in the police to catch the killers. Had this step been taken, mischief could have been nipped in the bud. But Mrs. Gandhi's Home Minister Zail Singh said 'no' and the lady sided with him against the man on the spot.

Now Zail Singh was an interesting man. He had lot of horse sense. He even made some devout Sikhs eat the droppings of horses believed to be descended from Guru Govind Singh's 'Neela Ghoda' (blue horse). But obviously both, Mrs. Gandhi and Zail Singh were more interested in dividing the Sikhs and crushing the Akali Dal than in peace and progress in Punjab.

In 1948, when one Madanlal had made an attempt on Gandhiji's life, Zail Singh said to Sardar Patel that Madan was a Sikh sent by Maharaja Faridkot. Sardar sent him to IGP, Delhi, who handed him over to Raghunath Sharma of Sadar Bazar police station. In the course of interrogation he admitted that he had wanted to avenge the Maharaja for sending him to jail for some thefts in the local Gurudwara. The police gave him a few slaps and sent him home! This man now became Mrs. Gandhi's chief adviser on Punjab.

Sardar Gurudev Singh, DC of Amritsar, had informed New Delhi that he could easily arrest Bhindranwale. But Mrs. Gandhi posted one lac troops in Punjab and organized a bloody assault on the Golden Temple just to show how brave and strong she was. She had lost full 24 by-elections in the preceding month. And she hoped her 'victory' over the Sikhs in Punjab would win her the next General Election. But in the process thousands of lives had been lost—including her own. The Sikh psyche had been wounded.

Punjab had been humiliated. The Army had suffered mutiny in some areas. And wonder of wonders, her Principal Secretary P.N. Dhar, who was in USA at the time, heard a "mysterious voice" on the phone on the midnight of Oct-30-31, 1984 announcing to him, "The killing of Indira". Even Dhar's brother-in-law in Delhi had, till then, known only about the shooting, (vide P.N. Dhar's *Indira Gandhi*, p. 318). Who were these foreigners waiting so eagerly to announce the murder of India's Prime Minister? In making war in Punjab, Mrs. Gandhi had allowed foreign forces to fish in India.

That all this violence was wholly unnecessary became clear when, in 1986, GoI cleared the Golden Temple of terrorists—under Operation Black Thunder—without the loss of any life. In the 1984 Operation Blue Star, the objective clearly was purely political, electoral.

Mrs. Gandhi's storming of the Golden Temple and destruction of Akal Takht in June 1984, had pained the country and scandalized the Sikhs. The following month an Indian Airlines plane flying from Chandigarh to Delhi was hijacked to Lahore. And the hijacking was done by a Sikh policeman who was doing guard duty at the residence of Law Minister Jagannath Kaushal! Ropar Canal had been breached. And hundreds of Sikh soldiers had mutinied, particularly in Bihar. There was, therefore, clear and present danger to the life of Mrs. Gandhi. On October 31, 1984, as many as four hundred and forty-four armed policemen, intelligence men and officers were on duty at the PM's House. And yet she was killed just like that. Here was a colossal failure of security. Any number of questions arise.

The danger to her life was so clear that Sikh security men in her set-up had been taken off that duty. But Mrs. Gandhi insisted on having them back—just to be able to show that all was well and that she fully trusted the Sikhs.

How is it that no senior security officer told her that that was not possible; that anything happening to her could have serious consequences for the whole country? The whole security apparatus stood paralysed. Mrs. Gandhi had her Sikh security men back for political show.

Mrs. Gandhi was shot dead by Beant Singh and Satwant Singh. Neither of them had their scheduled duty at that place and at that time. Both of them had their duty spot and duty time changed to the same spot and the same hour. How is it that no responsible security officer noted this very special simultaneous request for change of duty time and place? When a few years back US President Reagan was shot, his security man standing next to him immediately covered him. Reagan was hospitalized. His security man was disabled for life; but he had saved the President's life. How is it that nobody covered Mrs. Gandhi? Is it a fact that all the five people accompanying her—including Dhawan and Fotedar and the security men—literally fled in all directions?

Beant fired five revolver shots at her. Satwant emptied his 25 stengun shots into her. She fell down with a thud. The time was 9.12 a.m.

Beant and Satwant both threw their weapons to the ground and said: *"Hamne jo karna tha kar liya. Tumhe jo karna ho kar lo."*

Why was the mortally wounded PM put into an Ambassador car—and not in the ambulance always kept ready there?

Is it a fact that this car first moved in the direction of Ram Manohar Lohia Hospital, and only later changed course to the All India Institute of Medical Sciences?

Is it a fact that nobody had informed AIIMS what had happened and that they were coming?

Is it a fact that when the Ambassador car reached AIIMS

it found the wicket-gate closed and it had to smash its way in?

With thirty holes in her frail body, Mrs. Gandhi was gone. But they gave her 38 bottles of blood, until at 2.23 p.m. they realized that the body was rejecting the blood transfusion. They then disconnected the heart-lung machine. But even then they would not announce the end. Shri Vajpayee and Shri Advani, who rushed to AIIMS to find out what was happening, were nonchalantly told by Arun Nehru coming out of Operation Theatre: "She is out of danger."

Meanwhile Beant and Satwant had been taken to Indo-Tibetan Border Police Guard Room at the PM's House.

After a few minutes shots were heard from this Guard Room. According to ITBP's Subedar Tarseem Singh, Beant had got up to snatch his stengun, and so had Satwant. In the scuffle that ensued, he said, there was a burst of fire from his stengun which was kept in a ready position. Constable Ram Saran of ITBP fired from the gate of guard-room. Both Beant and Satwant fell in a heap on the ground.

Although the authorities have exonerated the ITBP, many questions arise. How could two unarmed men have snatched arms from well-trained armed men?

Assuming Beant and Satwant had attempted the impossible, why could not the ITBP men just disable them – and not shoot to kill them?

In the current case, Beant Singh was the main killer; he had chosen Satwant to be with him only because, as a constable, he was carrying a stengun. Beant Singh must have known much more about the conspiracy than Satwant. And now he was no more. On the night of October 30, only hours before the shooting, he had called up London and Vancouver. Who had he called – and why? Thanks to ITBP failure to keep Beant safe and secure, we will never know.

Satwant not only did not know about the conspiracy, he was first thinking of shooting Beant when the latter shot at Mrs. Gandhi, with a view to getting some reward from the department!

And now even Satwant had taken twelve shots and his condition was admittedly 'precarious' - with one bullet still lodged in his body.

While still in a critical condition he told his interrogators: "The security staff secured us and took us to ITBP Guard Room where we were made to sit on the chairs, and the Guards of ITBP took position, keeping their stenguns aimed at us. Some time later, the ITBP Guards opened fire at me and Beant Singh. Twelve bullets hit me, and Beant died at that very place. I also became unconscious and thereafter I was admitted to the hospital."

Truth, they say, sits on the lips of dying men. And Satwant Singh was dying at that time - though, mercifully for the Prosecution, he did not die at the time.

Obviously the ITBP action was **not** as innocent as it was made out to be by the authorities. Equally obviously there were powerful forces wanting to silence both, Beant and Satwant. Beant was dead, and now two attempts were made to reach Satwant, obviously to kill him. One person falsely claimed to be a resident doctor and another claimed to be a sweeper. However, unfortunately for the Prosecution, the two persons were not held and handed over to the police.

And curiously enough the Police Commissioner of Delhi ordered around 10 a.m., October 31, that the case may be investigated by the Homicide Squad of the Crime Branch, CID, instead of by the Tughlaq Road Police Station, in whose jurisdiction the case fell.

Ironically, the ambulance which was there for the PM, now carried her killers to the hospital! And Mr. Dhawan was making anxious inquiries about Beant Singh!

An even more basic question arises: Why were men with a very bad record like Beant and Satwant posted at the Prime Minister's House?

Beant had been recruited as sub-inspector in Delhi in 1971. He was awarded a censure in 1981 for the release of an accused person on a bogus security, produced by him. He was also charge-sheeted in 1981 for lapses in the investigation of a case of theft and recovery of a taxi, and this charge was still pending against him at the time of assassination. He had also come to adverse notice twice for insubordination and for habitual late-coming. He was also known to be a fun-loving person, addicted to many vices. He was even reported to his superior officers as unfit for continuation in the PM's security, and yet he continued to be there. Why?

Satwant had an even worse record. In the one year he spent in PM's security, he had as many as thirty-five minor punishments. His boss, Inspector Yogeshwar Sharma, had reported on July 27, 1984 to his superiors that Satwant, along with twelve other men, were unfit to continue in the PM's security. But here again no action was taken.

The Thakkar Commission inquiring into Mrs. Gandhi's murder, found that many members of the force with bad records were posted to the PM's security—more as a punishment than as a prestigious posting to man the security of the PM of the country.

The question arises: What was wrong with the Prime Minister's House that policemen should look upon duty there as punishment, and not as an honour?

Nor was that all. There was serious miscarriage of justice. The murder of a Prime Minister was serious enough to merit a special court—like Gandhi Murder case. But nothing of the kind was done. After evidence was concluded, it took one year to commence the arguments. The Supreme

Court set up a dubious record. In a day-to-day hearing, it spent three months hearing the **facts** of the case when the law limits it to hearing only points of law.

Since the case dragged on in the Sessions, High Court and Supreme Court for almost five long years, "the larger conspiracy" behind the assassination got slowed down. And so the charge-sheet in the larger conspiracy case was filed only on April 7, 1989. Had it been filed earlier, the defence would have asked for the clubbing of the two cases—and that would have only further delayed the murder case.

Funnily enough, though the accused were men of means, the Court provided these murderers with counsel at inflated fees—at public expense!

The Supreme Court even allowed the Defence Counsel to question at length the President's power to pardon or not to pardon!

The Press carried "disinformation" all the time - and it was never contradicted or corrected by the Government. Over a period of five years the Special Investigation Team expenses came to only Rs. 1.7 crores, much of it on lawyers for both Prosecution and Defence. But the media kept on saying it was a white elephant.

The SIT was particularly shocked that the Supreme Court should have acquitted Balbir Singh who had made a voluntary confession and whose guilt had been established on facts by the Sessions and High Courts.

But still worse was to follow. The second charge-sheet had already been laid. But Rajiv Gandhi, who had already lost the 1989 election, now decided to withdraw this case! At whose instance did he do this? Was he not interested in probing the larger conspiracy behind his mother's assassination? Or was he afraid it may throw up very inconvenient, very embarrassing facts? In any case what moral authority did a defeated PM have to close a case which

would have exposed the larger conspiracy against the country?

Mr. S. Anandram, IPS, who had been specially summoned from Hyderabad, to head the SIT, was shocked and "greatly affronted" by the decision. He therefore met Rajiv and expressed his unhappiness. So Rajiv told him: "Why don't you write a book and let the public know the full facts of the case?" Anandram decided there and then to do this book on the subject. But when he asked for records—which he himself had prepared at great risk to his life—to do an authentic account, he was refused. Anandram felt "humiliated" but he did not give up and he wrote *Assassination of a Prime Minister* (Vision Books). In the preface he noted that "Several matters came to the notice of SIT while investigating the case in depth"—matters which are now buried in SIT records. These records need to be preserved for posterity in the National Archives for, on them, depends the future security of the Indian State. However, enough has come out to show that the foreign hand was very active here.

There is no smoking gun but there are any number of guns—and any amount of smoke. You have only to put two and two together to see that this smoke comes from those guns in the West.

It was a British puppet, Chandhuri Rahmat Ali, who concocted the scheme of Partition—and Balkanisation--of India. Every Muslim-populated area and every Muslim-ruled state was to become a separate Sovereign State and the remaining 'India' itself was to be re-named 'Dinia', plural for 'Deen' or religion!

And now it was the British who formulated the theory—to the surprise of Sikhs no less than others that Sikhs were not Hindus. They even tried to persuade the Sikhs to opt for Pakistan in 1947. And when that trick also

failed, one Prof. Kapur Singh of Oxford University coined the word 'Khalistan' – something that no Sikh in India had asked for. But from then on London became the capital of 'Khalistan'.

This foreign inspired mischief started with the murder of Lala Jagat Narain, former senior minister and leading editor. His killer, Talwinder Singh Parmar, fled to Germany via Nepal. And a German Court sent him, not to India but to Canada, which western country again refused to extradite the murderer to India.

The unfortunate Operation Blue Star commenced on June 3, 1984. And on June 6, BBC Broadcast the appeal by Jagjit Singh Chauhan, so-called President of 'Khalistan', to kill Mrs. Gandhi, Rajiv Gandhi and the Generals. And they did kill them – including General Vaidya, Chief of Army Staff in 1984.

Chauhan not only proudly claimed credit for the assassination of Mrs. Gandhi, he celebrated it with a champagne party!

On June 11, thirty thousand Sikhs paraded the streets of London with naked swords. And the British Government not only permitted this obscenity, it provided police protection to Chauhan!

In the USA, Frank Capra of FBI conducted a regular school of sabotage for sundry terrorists. Secretary of State Henry Kissinger enunciated the Guam Doctrine to make "Asians fight Asians." The Tavistock Institute of Race Relations was set up to foment tribal and racial conflicts. And Triage Policy was adopted to curb non-white populations, by making developing countries dependent on imported food – in hopes of withholding the same at critical times, to bring them to their knees. CIA's Allen Dulles hoped to bring round India by alternately "sincerely loving it and sincerely deceiving it".

CIA had got many world leaders—Che Guevara of Cuba, Patrice Lumumba of Congo, Allende of Chile—assassinated. The US Ambassador in India, Patrick Moynihan, in a confidential note to Kissinger told him that recent reports of CIA activities had confirmed Mrs. Gandhi's "worst suspicions and genuine fears" about American intentions towards India. He added: "She knows fully well that we have done our share and more of bloody and dishonourable deeds."

Time magazine reported that Moynihan had angrily called the State Department that he had assured Mrs. Gandhi that CIA had not been involved in the Chilean coup. Now (in view of American admission) she wondered "whether India might not be the next" on the list.

Reporting President Ford's admission of American assassination of foreign leaders, *Time* said: "It left the troubling impression that the USA feels free to subvert another Government wherever it suits American policy."

The Wall Street Journal and the *New York Times* reported in March 1975 that the CIA Director, William Colby, had admitted to President Ford that CIA had plotted assassination attempts on several foreign leaders. Senator Frank Church (D) of Idaho, Chairman Senate Intelligence Committee said: "It tantamounts to saying that we respect no law save the law of the jungle."

The US State Department even commissioned a special study on what would happen if Mrs. Gandhi were to die suddenly. Since she was in excellent health, sudden death could only mean unnatural death, that is assassination. Here the American wish for her death was father to the thought.

This study was done by one Robert L. Hardgrave Jr., under the title *India Under Pressure: Prospects for Political Stability*. The study was done in 1983 and the book itself was published in June 1984. Obviously the US State

Department was toying with the idea of Mrs. Gandhi's killing even before 'Blue Star'. *Patriot* of Delhi published this story on December 16, 1984—just six weeks after her killing.

On page 113 of this book, the author even hopefully foresaw an "inevitable sympathy vote" for Rajiv. And in the event of Rajiv not getting a secure majority "India might then enter a period of prolonged instability" when "the military will intervene and send the politicians packing". Democratic America loves military dictators.

Mrs. Gandhi could see what was coming and, in a public speech on August 6, she cited "a Washington, D.C. based espionage agency" and said: "The demand for Khalistan did not come from anywhere inside India, not even, in fact, from the Sikh political party, the Akali Dal or even Bhindranwale. The demand came only from certain people settled abroad, at the instigation of foreign agencies."

And when Mrs. Gandhi was struck down, US General Milnor Roberts (Retd.) presiding over a conference of 'Khalistanis', Kashmiri separatists, Tamil separatists and 'Afghan Jehadis' in London, did not attempt to hide his enthusiasm. He was even pleased that "It will certainly take the pressure off Pakistan."

Neither UK nor USA can disown their responsibility for the mayhem in Punjab—and the assassination of Mrs. Gandhi.

□

Kanishka

June 23, 1985, was a very sad day for India. Air India's Boeing 747, *Kanishka*, was on its way from Toronto and Montreal in Canada, to Bombay and Delhi, India. And then it suddenly disappeared from radar screens. It had blown up and sunk into the Atlantic, 160 km off the Irish coast. India had not only lost a big plane, Indian tourism had received a body blow. Three hundred and twenty nine passengers and crew had met their fiery-watery grave. It was the deadliest case of aerial sabotage. India-Canada air service was suspended for years. It was an assault on India.

Government of India appointed Justice Kirpal to inquire into the matter. Since the plane wreckage was resting two miles deep into the sea, only some 5% of it could be retrieved. Some shameless people even published a book, *Soft Target*, saying that India had deliberately blown its own plane, just to give Canadian Khalistanis a bad name. Some others claimed that the plane could have gone to pieces as a result of engine failure or metal fatigue. However, the Boeing people made it clear that no Boeing plane had ever crashed like this. And meanwhile divers recovered a bag containing the remnants of the bomb, the metal skin of the fuselage and other physical evidence. Blast signatures like holes with tongues of metal curled outwards and spikes on the fracture

edges confirmed the findings of National Aeronautical Laboratory, Bangalore, and Bhabha Atomic Research Centre, Mumbai, that it was an act of sabotage. At the same time another Khalistani bomb attempt on an Air India plane had killed two Japanese handlers at Narita airport, Tokyo, and Inderjit Singh Reyat, a Khalistani from Canada, was duly sentenced for this to ten years for 'man-slaughter'.

However, this was only the beginning of the story. *Kanishka* incident had hurt India; but it had embarrassed Canada even more, for it indicated security failure at Canadian airports. Canadian authorities therefore went to work.

All honour to Canada that it spent $60 million to investigate the matter. It even announced $1 million prize for information leading to the unravelling of the plot. And it got some good leads. More recently it spent $5 million to re-equip its court room, complete with bullet-proof glass, to pre-empt any attempt at escape by the rich, influential and unscrupulous men now standing trial in Vancouver. (These people are also involved in a tax fraud case of $16.25 million in Canada.) But let me not anticipate.

The Royal Canadian Mounted Police, in charge of this case, surprised the world when, almost ten years after the event, in 1994, it unravelled the mystery. *The Globe and Mail* and the Canadian Broadcasting Corporation with its 'Fifth Estate' programme, now revealed that four Canadian Khalistanis had done it. And they had been trained in sabotage in a School for Sabotage run by FBI agent Frank Camper in Birmingham, Alabama, USA. Two years after the incident, Camper told the US Senate Intelligence Committee: "I told the FBI about their plan but FBI had refused to notify India. The militants were deadly serious to raise hell in India. On June 23, 1985 I was literally sick in my stomach. But I was told by FBI not to answer any

question if the Canadian intelligence were to interrogate me. For Air India bombing would have implicated Pakistan."

CIA Director Gate told the Senate Intelligence Committee: "I cannot tell you what I was aware of, as our focus that time was towards Afghanistan and getting the Soviets out." Canadian Intelligence confirmed that "Neither the FBI nor the CIA provided any useful assistance during the investigation of Air India bombing." Since Pakistan was helping USA in Afghanistan, USA decided to help Pakistan hurt India!

In the light of the above a question was raised in the Rajya Sabha (unstarred Q. No. 1038 dated 2.3.1994):

Shri K.R. Malkani

"Will the Minister of External Affairs be pleased to state:

"(a) whether Government have taken note of *The Globe and Mail*, Canada, report that the CIA and FBI knew before hand of the planned bombing of Air India's airliner *Kanishka* in 1985, costing 329 lives, by extremist Sikhs in league with Pakistan;

"(b) if so, whether it is a fact that they did not communicate this information either to India or to Canada;

"(c) whether Government have protested to the US Government against this grave sin of omission on the part of its secret agencies; and

"(d) whether it will consider asking the US for apology in the matter and for paying the due compensation for losses suffered?"

The Minister of State for External Affairs, Shri R.L. Bhatia's reply was:

"(a) Yes, Sir.

"(b) Government have received adequate cooperation from US Agencies in matters pertaining to terrorist activities targeting India. Government have no evidence to conclude that information as alleged in the Canadian Broadcasting Corporation-TV documentary and reported in *The Globe and Mail,* was available with the US Government.

"(c) Does not arise.

"(d) Does not arise."

In my letter of 7.3.1994, I wrote to Shri Bhatia:

"Dear Shri Bhatia:

"Please refer to your Answer to my unstarred Question No. 1038 of March 2, 1994.

"You have said in this reply that Government have no evidence to conclude that information as alleged in the C.B.C. TV documentary and reported in *The Globe and Mail,* was available with the US Government".

"I am afraid your answer evades the Question.

"According to the above report this information was available with FBI and CIA - and the two agencies are integral parts of the US Government.

"If the Government of India doubt the truth of the Canadian report why has it made copies of the same available to senior Indian journalists?"

"Yours sincerely,
"(K.R. Malkani)"

And in his reply dated April 21, 1994, Shri Bhatia said:

"Please refer to your letter of March 7, 1994 regarding the reply provided by this Ministry to your Unstarred Question No. 1038 of March 2, 1994. Having reviewed the matter carefully, I have to reiterate that Government have no evidence to conclude that information as alleged in the

CBC TV documentary and reported in *The Globe and Mail* was available with the US Government. We received adequate cooperation from the US agencies in regard to terrorist activities against India and we have no basis whatever for assuming that US Agencies or the US Government withheld any relevant information in their possession during the *Kanishka* investigation."

USA's FBI agents were training Khalistani saboteurs to raise hell in India. And the Government of India claims USA was cooperating with India! Can illusion go farther? Nor was UK very cooperative. When Canada asked for extradition of Ryet to stand trial for *Kanishka*, it hemmed and hawed and took its own time.

Even more serious was the attitude of Canada's own Security Intelligence Service. The CSIS seemed to be closer to CIA and FBI than to Canada's own RCMP. CSIS had some 300 tapes covering the sinister activities of Khalistanis in Canada. But all but 54 of these were erased as early as 1995—to destroy the evidence against murderous Khalistanis!

CSIS had a mole among Khalistanis, Surjan Singh Gill. Gill was a close friend of anti-extremists Tara Singh Hayer, editor-publisher of the *Indo-Canadian Times*. He had told Tara Singh how the *Kanishka* bomb was planted. And Tara Singh had published the news. The same night in 1998, Tara Singh was gunned down! Earlier, CSIS withdrew a valuable informant like Gill three days before *Kanishka* blew up. Key witness Gill has been sent away to Pakistan. Why, by whom—and at whose instance?

Today the *Kanishka* case is going on in Vancouver. Hundred and fifty journalists from a dozen countries are covering this sensational case. The happy thing to note is that eight hundred witnesses—many of them Canadian Sikhs—have come forward to give evidence against the saboteurs. Earlier, moderate Sikhs ousted extremists from the Board of two important Vancouver Gurdwaras. Ryet has been let off with a 5-year sentence in a plea-bargain in the *Kanishka* case; obviously he will be an approver in the case. The prosecution, therefore, is confident of securing convictions. But the fact that *Kanishka* could be blown up and its saboteurs blatantly protected by the USA, its allies and agents, should make us sit up when dealing with that country.

□

Rajiv: Questions, Questions All the Way

Rajiv Gandhi became Prime Minister of India. Perhaps his sole qualification for that office was the fact that his mother had been Prime Minister; and his grandfather had also been Prime Minister. As an Indian Airlines pilot, he had been very polite to passengers. He looked clean and was expected to be clean. As pilot, his readings had been confined to comics and thrillers. As Prime Minister, if given a 2-page note, he would ask why it could not be just two paras or just two sentences. He could even come up with Looney tunes. He once urged Hindu-Muslim amity, as in the days of Rama.

On the positive side, he had come up with the Punjab and the Assam accords. He lost the 1989 election and was engaged in the 1991 election campaign when he was assassinated at Sriperumbudur, Tamil Nadu, on May 21. Some people want the country to believe that he was poised to win the 1991 election and that the LTTE killed him because he had been rough with them and they didn't want to see him in power again.

The factual position is very different. Rajiv's Congress Party was expected to lose. And but for some sympathy wave generated by his killing—and by the cynical *asthi* processions by his party candidates—Congress would have won 30-50 seats less. And it would have been in no position to muster a near-majority and then convert it into a bare majority with the purchase of some more M.Ps.

It is significant that the Chandra Shekhar Cabinet, then in power with Congress support, met on May 22 to discuss not Rajiv killing but whether the Lok Sabha election, already more than half way through, should be cancelled and the Shekhar Government continue indefinitely.

A similar situation had earlier existed in Algeria. Here the general election was almost complete. The Nationalist Party dubbed 'Islamics' was poised to sweep the polls. At this stage the Army, at the instance of certain foreign powers, cancelled the election and let the military dictatorship continue. And it continues to this day!

Fortunately Indian democracy was too well rooted, and the Indian Army too civil and non-political to allow such a coup to materialise in India. But the sinister tragedy of May 21, 1991 was certainly an effort in that direction.

It has been argued that USA was not happy with Rajiv because he had doubled the Indian Defence budget, visited Russia and Iran—no friend of USA—and half objected to refuelling of US war planes during the Gulf War.

Well, hardly. Higher defence budget means more arms orders, and USA is by far the biggest arms trader. Visiting Russia was routine with Indian leaders. And even US leaders were visiting Iran on the sly. And as for refuelling, all Indian leaders in and around power at the time—whether Chandra Shekhar, Gujral or Rajiv—were in two minds. No, this could not be the reason for Rajiv's killing.

Rajiv was, like Reagan, an 'amiable dunce'. Some people here and abroad might have liked to have a stronger man, more firmly committed to them, to take his place. And

even more than that they obviously wanted to cancel the elections, derail Indian democracy and instal a civilian or military dictatorship *a la* say, Pakistan, to toe their line all along the line. A former Congress General Secretary told me that the then US Ambassador in India had told him that their first choice for Prime Minister of India was Subramaniam Swamy.

There is, however, no doubt that the actual killers of Rajiv were LTTE men. And the Government of India was as much responsible for it as the Government of Sri Lanka, apart from the foreign forces disturbing political waters from time to time to fish in them.

There was a time early in the nineteenth century when Sri Lanka was part of the Indian State. Apart from the old tribal people of the island, Sinhalese (73.8%) came from Eastern India some two thousand years ago, Sri Lanka Tamils (12.7%) came and settled in Jaffna in the north centuries ago, plantation-working Tamils (5.5%) came in the last century and then there are Muslims (7.1%). (Religion-wise there are 67.4% Buddhists, 17.6% Hindus, 7.9% Christians and 7.1% Muslims.) When the British occupied Sri Lanka, Tamils took to English education in a big way and before long they dominated the services and the professions. The Sinhalese resented this. Tamilians now needed to score 25% more marks for admission to professional institutions. Before long they declined from 40% to 15% in the professions.

When Sri Lanka became free, they declared Sinhala the national official language. Governments would sign agreements with Tamils only to go back on them under public pressure. (Although Buddhism is a religion of peace and non-violence, many Buddhist families make their difficult son a Bhikshu. The Buddhist clergy in Sri Lanka, therefore, can be quite difficult. They killed their Prime

Minister Bandarnaike.) In 1973, Sinhala police broke into the World Tamil Conference and indulged in loot and arson. On top of this, Afghan, Pakistan and even some Indian opium began to flow into Sri Lanka for onward worldwide trade. And the Tamil mafia in Madras and Jaffna was very much in it. The fat was fully in the fire.

Here was a ticklish situation that needed to be handled with the greatest care. But here both Governments failed. In India there was a general sympathy with Jaffna Tamils. But we forgot that LTTE was engaged in drug trade. And we forgot also that in 1975, LTTE men had killed Duraiappa, Mayor of Jaffna, just because he would not toe their line.

Sri Lanka retaliated by now supporting some Kashmiris' demand for self-determination. It also started buying arms and taking arms training in a number of countries. Instead of halting and reversing the mounting tensions, New Delhi crossed the *Lakshman Rekha* and started arming, training and financing Sri Lankan Tamils. At one stage we had thirty training camps in Tamil Nadu alone. It was an act of war against Sri Lanka. We once sent supplies to Jaffna against the wishes of Colombo. And when the Sri Lanka navy stopped us, we sent these supplies by air.

Unable to cope with the situation, Sri Lanka asked India to come over and discipline LTTE. And like a fool we walked straight into the trap. We signed the Indo-Sri Lanka Accord on July 29, 1987—and on July 30 our troops were in Sri Lanka. We failed to take note of the fact that while President Jayawardene was for the Accord, Prime Minister Premdasa was opposed to it. Nor did we take the attack on Rajiv by a Sri Lanka naval member of the Guard of Honour as a serious warning of worse to come.

To begin with, both Sri Lanka Freedom Party, the ruling party, and LTTE welcomed the Indian Peace-keeping Force. But within days both sides turned hostile. LTTE saw IPKF

as a friend turned-foe, and SLFP saw it as an army of occupation! LTTE refused to surrender arms to Sri Lanka Army. And Colombo refused to honour General Amnesty decision. On top of all this LTTE felt that in guaranteeing the territorial integrity of Sri Lanka, the accord closed the door on Eelam, a separate State of Tamils in Sri Lanka. The presence of IPKF also denied LTTE the status of sole spokesman and sole protector of Tamils in Sri Lanka. LTTE therefore started fighting IPKF! And Sri Lankans congratulated "our Tamil boys" for stopping the Indian Army in its tracks!

The humiliation of India was complete. The Indian Army suffered not only grievous injury but also gross insult. IPKF had 17 officers, 26 JCOs and 276 other ranks killed. IPKF wounded included 53 officers, 67 JCOs and 919 ORs. LTTE had 1100 killed. In 1990-93, Sri Lanka had 3000 soldiers killed; another 8000 deserted. All this thanks to the follies of two Governments and the mischief of sundry foreign forces.

More than two Indian Army Divisions were sent but since there was no mobilisation and no cancellation of leaves, only half the soldiers were in place. As against 130-150 artillery guns needed per battalion, the IPKF units rarely exceeded 3-6 guns. And while the bulk of IPKF forces were in Trincomalee area, attack was mounted in Jaffna area. LTTE shot down an IPKF helicopter, killing thirty-four commandos! More. While LTTE was fighting IPKF, our RAW was continuing its military aid to it! LTTE casualties were being treated in Indian hospitals!

Also, you can fight the opponent if you really hate him. How could Indian soldiers fire on Sri Lankan Tamilians who are like fellow-Indian Tamilians? Chief of Army Staff, General Sunderji behaved irresponsibly when he rushed troops to Sri Lanka without due preparation. But Rajiv behaved even more irresponsibly when he did not listen to the Army Lt. Gen. Depinder Singh. Overall Force Commander, IPKF, asked COAS why the Army point of view was not being heard and the latter revealed: *Woh Sunta Nahi Hai!* (he – i.e. Rajiv – does not listen!)

While all this was most unfortunate it had little to do with Rajiv's murder. Some elements, local and foreign, had decided to kill him for their own reasons. Some Khalistanis could also have done it but the violent anti-Sikh reaction to Indiraji's killing deterred them from a repeat provocation. They, therefore, decided on Tamil Nadu where LTTE is something more than political. And apart from native sympathy, it has a vast criminal network of drugs and arms dealers. In just one LTTE safe house in Coimbatore, belonging to one Dr. Gopal Krishnan, the police found one million detonators!

The assassination of Rajiv has cost the LTTE dearly. They have lost the sympathy, support and safe bases in India. But the financial and military support of some foreign countries has made LTTE the tallest terrorist organisation in the world. Apart from $ 84 million in cash, it has half a dozen deep sea-going ships, anti-aircraft guns, stringer missiles, even a submarine! Why Sivarasan even had a powerful wireless set with a range of a thousand kilometres and a 60-foot high antenna for it at Kedungaiyur, Madras.

It has been said that SPG cover should not have been removed after Rajiv ceased to be Prime Minister. That is right. It has also been said that there should have been NSG cover. However Justice Verma, who inquired into the security aspect, said that a security complement of 240 persons was "comprehensive and adequate". In any case, even Punjab Chief Minister Beant Singh with NSG cover was blown up right in front of the Secretariat. Here the problem was that the temple tank bed was a wrong site

for the meeting. The barricading material was very short. NSG or SPG does not look after these matters; the Police is supposed to. And this was neither the first nor the last failure of Tamil Nadu Police in the Rajiv case.

The tragedy of the situation is that when powerful forces are out to get you they can always get you. They can always choose the time and the place. And so even Kennedy could not escape it. In this particular case, LTTE had sent a 500 member killer squad. If Dhanu had failed with her waist bomb, some other killer would have done it. As soon as the blast took place, a white Ambassador with two white men sped away flashing its revolving red light, a blue Ambassador which had screeched to a halt just behind the dais minutes before Rajiv's arrival, with its tinted glasses rolled up, followed suit.

The best course for Rajiv would have been *not* to go to Tamil Nadu. Mahant Sewa Das had been sent to London by Prime Minister Chandra Shekhar in December 1990, to persuade Jagjit Singh Chauhan to call off the Punjab mayhem. He came back and reported meeting at Chauhan's place (64 Western Court, Central London) LTTE, Sikhistan and JKLF terrorists, telling him "*Rajiv to gaya.*" When Rajiv heard all this he began to sweat even in Delhi's February. With Rajiv not scheduled to go to Kashmir, and with Khalistanis lying low, LTTE was the obvious threat. Since Congress-AIADMK combine was doing very well in Tamil Nadu and the local Congress candidate Mrs. Margatham Chandrashekhar had never asked him to visit her constituency, there was no reason for Rajiv to go to Sriperumbudur and that too at two days' notice by AICC. Perhaps Sonia Gandhi could have thrown some light on this matter. But she did not appear before the Jain Commission.

Neena Gopal who was with Rajiv from Chennai on and changed to another car only minutes before

Sriperumbudur, told me that people enroute were banging the car and even abusing him but Rajiv thought they were only being enthusiastic in welcoming him. At places he was shaking hands through the window and they were even pulling him out at unscheduled points.

Neena who is from Kerala but understands Tamil, told him: "Are you not dicing with death?" But Rajiv did not understand and no Tamil Congressman or security man took any preventive or protective action. The rest, as they say, is history.

Rajiv Sharma, in his book aptly titled *Beyond the Tigers,* writes: "Laxmi, the librarian at the Indian High Commission in Colombo, had a mysterious call nearly six hours before the assassination.

'Is Rajiv dead', the caller asked in chaste English. Laxmi, a Sri Lankan Tamil, asked the caller to identify himself, but he had already hung up. She took it as a prank and did not inform anybody about it, until the next day when she realised its importance.

"Was the anonymous caller a friend or a foe? Did he want to tip off Indian Intelligence agencies about the coming event or was he a desperate conspirator or accomplice who wanted to check their secret mission's progress?" (p. 10)

(Mrs. Gandhi's Principal Private Secretary had a similar mysterious call when she was shot dead on October 30, 1984. In his book *Indira Gandhi, Emergency & Indian Democracy,* he writes that he was in the USA and his brother-in-law in Delhi had only confirmed the shooting. But this midnight mysterious voice announced her death – and hung up! (p. 318) What has been happening?

The Government appointed Justice Verma Commission to report on the security failure(s) if any. And it held Tamil Nadu Police, State Government, I.B. and Union Home Ministry responsible in varying degrees. (I had some

revealing experience with Tamil Nadu Police in Coimbatore. Here on February 16, 1998, at the venue of Advaniji's meeting there were nine explosions taking 25 lives in just fifteen minutes. Shri Advaniji was saved only by God's grace because his flight was late by an hour. And yet when we met top police officers they were just smiling away!)

Since the Verma Commission was appointed to report only on the security aspect, the demand went up to probe the conspiracy aspect. But it would seem the Government was not interested in unravelling the truth, the whole truth and nothing but the truth. And so all kinds of strange things began to happen. File after crucial file was found missing or doctored. Witness after crucial witness began to die. Vinod Pande, Cabinet Secretary in the V.P. Singh Government deposed before the Jain Commission that file no. 8-1-WR/JSS/90 Vol. III - in which he had made notings on Rajiv Gandhi's security - had been tampered with. "The file which has been placed in my hands does not contain an office copy of my note dated January 30, 1990. The first five paras of the draft note are not mine." Files disappeared even from PMO! Who was doing all this?

Although a big foreign hand was suspected from day one, IED (Improved Explosive Device) and the deliberately blurred video of the assassination were sent to foreign countries like Israel and USA for examination. And nothing was heard of them again.

Vijay Karan, CBI Chief, was shocked to find that somebody had made Hari Babu's photographs of Dhanu, Sivarasan and other key members of the killer group available to the press. When Sivarasan saw these in the newspapers he became doubly careful. The police instead of capturing 27 of them holed up in Konakunte, Bangalore in a surprise raid, waited for more police which was not even needed. When the police at last stormed the place they could find only seven bodies. The other twenty had evaporated in thin air!

The suicide of Shanmugam, key smuggler-cum-LTTE terrorist was even more scandalous. This man was caught and he gave much useful information. But his uncle, Seetharaman, obviously a bigger agent, was allowed by SIT to meet him in complete privacy for a whole hour. After his meal, instead of washing his hands in the basin close by, he was allowed to go behind the building. His body was found only eight hours later. Why did Karthikeyan take away Shanmugam from the care of officers who had captured him and hand him over to Sri Kumar, a DIG from Delhi who was not even a member of SIT at the time? And this same Sri Kumar 'lost' the crucial brief case at London airport!

Sivarasan and his friends had sought shelter in the house of one Ranganath in Bangalore. Ranganath was one of the accused in the Rajiv murder case. When he was acquitted, he said he would tell everything. Did the police ever get his statement? If yes, where is it? If not, why not? Although the two Commission Reports show that investigation is not complete; SIT Chief Karthikeyan kept saying that investigation was complete and therefore, there will be no supplementary charge-sheet. SIT even made the explosives expert Major Sabharwal of the National Security Guards to change his report that Dhanu's belt bomb had three Singapore-made grenades in it, and not one. Mercifully, Sabharwal's original report is still available with NSG.

On the night of March 5-6, 1991, RAW intercepted a coded message from Sivarasan to LTTE's Pottu Ammani in Jaffna asking whether Rajiv was to be killed in Madras or Delhi. This message was decoded only six months later, when Rajiv was already long dead! Reason: The chief

decoder of RAW was on one month's leave!

It is obvious that there were influential people who did not want the whole nasty truth to come out. Actually two special leave petitions were sponsored by the Government to have the Jain Commission wound up. However, Chief Justice Ahmedi and Justice Bharucha of the Supreme Court dismissed them.

When Rajiv was killed, Seshan, who had been his Security Secretary, told Swamy that he suspected foreign hand in it. Thereupon, writes Govindan Kutty in his biography of Seshan, Swamy was "possessed by anger".

"What he blurted out as he slammed the door behind him, sounded like a warning. For he told Seshan that if his fears and suspicions were true he could also be logically in danger if he voiced those suspicions publicly." The following day, Swamy "renewed his warning". Says Kutty "A hundred questions slithered through Seshan's mind." But these suspicions of a former security chief were never forwarded to SIT for a proper probe!

Swamy was all for arms for LTTE and partition of Sri Lanka. Rohan Gunaratne in his book *The Indian Intervention in Sri Lanka* confirmed that Swamy had arranged LTTE training with Mossad, the Israeli Intelligence Organisation. No wonder LTTE began to get arms from Israel when that country did not have even an Embassy in Colombo!

But Swamy now accused Minister of State Margaret Alva of being close to LTTE! Since Swamy, though not even an M.P. had been given Cabinet rank—as in-charge of labour problems under WTO!—she sought Narasimha Rao's permission to sue Swamy for defamation. The permission never came. (That Rao had appointed Swamy in charge of 'Labour under WTO' without consulting Labour Minister Sangma, and all the Trade Unions refused to see Swamy, is another story.)

Interestingly enough the CBI and SIT were sure that it was LTTE – and LTTE alone. And External Affairs Ministry and RAW agreed with them. RAW filed an affidavit before the Jain Commission on September 15, 1993, stating that it has "no information, material evidence, oral or documentary, to substantiate the alleged involvement of Mossad and CIA in the assassination of Shri Rajiv Gandhi..... The theory of external plot could not be substantiated."

One can understand New Delhi's anxiety **not** to confront Washington. As Bob Woodward, senior American journalist writes in his book *VEIL. The Secret War of the CIA – 1981-1987*: "CIA sources in India had been compromised and rolled up; Indian Prime Minister Indira Gandhi had been furious that the United States had a spy in her midst. But both countries had decided to play down the matter." (p. 310). According to this book, Government of India received stunning proof of a US strategic plan to 'Balkanise India.'

Discretion can be the better part of valour. But truth is above both, discretion and valour. And the truth here is that even Narasimha Rao described Rajiv's assassination as a larger "design by divisive forces to destabilise the country." Shri V.N. Gadgil, M.P. and Congress spokesman said the assassination of Rajiv was "part of an international conspiracy and showed how far the CIA's hands have stretched." Earlier, the Thakkar Natarajan Commission inquiring into V.P. Singh's Fairfax Case, had noted: "In brief, the CIA has and will continue to conduct mayhem throughout the world regardless of law or accepted norms."

Major General Afsir Karim says, "We have been sitting atop a volcano... The long-term strategy of the LTTE is to create a 'Pan-Dravida-Nadu', joining Tamil Nadu with the Tamil regions of Sri Lanka ... LTTE wants to, and already has to some extent, developed a symbiotic relationship with all separatist or terrorist groups in India, in order to facilitate the smuggling of weapons and to trade in narcotics" (*Transnational Terrorism: The Danger in the South*, Lancer, p. 65). It is significant that USA has installed itself in Diego Garcia which is nearer to Chennai than Chennai is to Delhi.

Vijay Karan, CBI Chief at the time, says the question that seems to rankle in the minds of many is: "Does the conspiracy stop with Prabhakaran and the LTTE or are there others? Or is there a wider conspiracy that has still not been unravelled?... I do not rule out the possibility of involvement of various external forces in the assassination."

One month before the incident, four Ambassadors in Tunis had conveyed the information from Yasser Arafat that during the election period Rajiv's enemies would get rid of him. Zafar Saifullah, Cabinet Secretary in the mid-nineties, told the Commission that during his office he had been given intercepts of Mossad communication that implicated Israel in the assassination. He added that these intercepts were subsequently found missing or were destroyed by a successor government. Former Foreign Secretary Muchkund Dubey said that prior information of the assassination plot may refer to Mossad and could even be CIA. Another former Foreign Secretary, J.N. Dixit, said that the CIA was a hostile force. And yet another former Foreign Secretary, G.S. Bajpai, told the Commission: "On June 4, 1991, Prime Minister Chandra Shekhar told me that he had been told by Yasser Arafat that CIA/Mossad/LTTE were behind the plot to kill Rajiv Gandhi."

The Mossad – a close ally of CIA – took us all for a nice ride. While they supplied PT boats to Sri Lanka they provided anti-PT boats to LTTE. At one stage Mossad was simultaneously giving some specialised training to LTTE, Sri Lanka and – India!

Interesting information also came from the political

leadership. Rajani Ranjan Sahu, M.P., informed Justice Jain that he met Jitendra Prasad, Political Secretary to Narasimha Rao, Subramaniam Swamy and journalist Rajiv Shukla in the Raj Bhavan on the occasion of the marriage of Jayant Malhotra's son in Bangalore. Here Swamy had told them that Prabhakaran could not have killed Rajiv out of animosity, but only for big money amounting to hundreds of crores.

The most important statement of course, came from the then Home Minister Shri S.B. Chavan. On June 4, 1991, he told the House that a superpower was behind Rajiv's assassination. Since there has been only one superpower in the world since 1990, the reference was clear. That very day the American Ambassador met the Prime Minister, the Foreign Minister and the Foreign Secretary. After that the spokesman of the Ministry of External Affairs held a Press Conference to contradict the Home Minister's statement. (In a parallel situation, during the 1965 Indo-Pakistan War, we had destroyed and captured many Patton tanks supplied to Pakistan by USA. We even displayed a captured Patton tank in New Delhi. USA did not like it. It took it as an insult—and an injury to its arms trade. In this situation Shri Lal Bahadur Shastri withdrew the Patton tank from display.)

Later Shri Chavan 'corrected' himself to say: "I made that statement on the basis of my general impression." He added: "I made a mistake while mentioning the word 'superpower' which should have been ' some foreign powers'. There is only one super-power left." But he also said: "It is abnormal that the spokesperson of the Ministry of External Affairs should have held the Press Conference contradicting my statement." And he said that important files had been kept away from him.

In his native goodness Chavan even justified holding

back certain documents because they may "malign a family." But he misunderstood the very purport of an inquiry into a VVIP murder. The idea is to get at the truth, the whole truth and nothing but the truth—and not to malign or align any family.

In this ticklish situation Justice Jain tried to balance himself on the horns of the Government dilemma. He said he found the theory of involvement of foreign agency to be incredible in material aspects. But he also said that in view of the lethal high-tech weaponry of LTTE, "the possibility of a foreign hand behind the LTTE can't be ruled out, rather it is strengthened." And he added: "The conspiracy as to who was responsible for the assassination of the Father of the Nation—not the particular Nathuram Godse who pulled the trigger—remains yet to be unveiled." By implication he obviously meant that the conspiracy behind Rajiv's assassination also remained to be unveiled. But again in a bid not to irritate USA he pointed the accusing finger only at "segments of the US defence and intelligence establishment"—as though CIA is not part of US Government! (It reminded me of the blowing up of Air India's *Kanishka* by some Khalistani students of an FBI School for Sabotage. When asked if USA had informed us of the danger, Rao Government's response was: yes the FBI knew it but we do not know if US Government knew it!)

Verily, truth can be stranger than fiction. And one can only hope that it answers the questions raised by Rajiv's mysterious murder.

□

PURULIA:
"Weapons from Heaven"

On December 23, 1995, the country was surprised to hear that a 'mystery plane' had been force-landed at Mumbai airport after "high drama" over the Indian skies. And it was shocked to learn that this same plane had air-dropped a huge consignment of lethal weaponry in Purulia, West Bengal, on the night of December 17-18. These weapons included not only hundreds of AK-47/56 rifles but 9 rocket-launchers, 81 anti-tank grenades, thousands of 7.62 MM and 9 MM ammunition and all else needed by a whole battalion of troops. Here were one hundred boxes weighing 96 kg each, air-dropped by five or more huge parachutes with a diameter of fifty to sixty feet! Here were ninety tonnes of armaments, costing Rs. 35 crores, injected into the industrial heart of India next to Ranchi, Bokaro and Dhanbad. (The villagers in Purulia area said the armaments boxes fell with heavy thuds and there were also some loud explosions "like a bomb".)

The Directorate-General of Civil Aviation had permitted the plane to over-fly India from Pakistan to Bangladesh and Myanmar, halting in Varanasi only for re-fuelling. Actually the plane not only halted in Varanasi, but also in Kolkata. And while it was to return to Karachi via Kolkata, it landed up in Chennai and would have escaped to Pakistan, had not two MIG-21 fighters threatened to shoot it down if it did not land in Mumbai. The warning words were: "You will be leaving Indian airspace at the risk of your own health."

The whole thing stunned the country. Prime Minister P.V. Narasimha Rao was reported "fuming". And Shri Vajpayee, then Leader of Opposition, said the Purulia arms air-drop case showed that an international conspiracy is being hatched to instigate a civil war in India. The BJP appointed a four-MP Committee consisting of Sarvashri Vishnu Kant Shastri, Rita Verma, Gen. Khanduri and K.R. Malkani to visit Purulia, surrounding areas and Kolkata and report the situation. Before leaving for Purulia the team met Home Minister S.B. Chavan who was worried about the whole thing and said there must have been at least five parachutes but only two had been found.

From December 18 to December 23, the coal mafia and other elements in the adjoining industrial belt of Bihar had had enough time to seize and hide at least one-third of the weaponry. And now the DIG of West Bengal gave the villagers four more days to surrender the arms. No wonder nobody turned in anything. When the BJP team visited the affected Purulia area on December 27 we could not see a single policeman doing anything anywhere. Evidently they were busy with the security of Minister of State, Home, Syed Sibte Razi, who had also decided to visit Purulia the same day as BJP team.

When asked why helicopters had not been used to locate the huge arms and ammo boxes and the parachutes, we were told that West Bengal had only two copters and both were in the garage, awaiting repairs.

West Bengal Home Secretary Manish Gupta said it was

an international conspiracy and they knew who had sent the arms and for whom, but he would not elaborate. But the facts of the case revealed quite a bit.

According to Aircraft Rules of India, no aircraft, Indian or foreign, can carry weapons over Indian air space. AN-26 is known to be a military cargo aircraft. How did DGCA permit AN-26 to cross Indian air-space?

Also is it a fact that DGCA did *not* inform Home or Defence about this weapons flight? Incidentally it was so heavily loaded that it could not fly low to avoid being seen on radar screen.

Why did Chennai allow it to land when it had permission to proceed to Pakistan only via Kolkata?

The AN-26 left Karachi on December 17 at 1.42 PM. It reached Varanasi at 5.42 PM after four hours. Karachi-Varanasi would take only about two hours. What was it doing in the Indian skies for the remaining time?

It left Varanasi at 10 PM and reached Kolkata at 12.45 AM, December 18, a distance of only 45 minutes. Did it spend two hours over Purulia? Or did it play some other games also?

Bangladesh and Myanmar, which were supposed to be the destinations of this AN-26's cargo, refused it permission to land in Dhaka or Yangon. It then left for Phuket, Thailand. On December 21, it landed in Chennai at 8.45 AM—and left at 10.45 PM. But it reached Mumbai only at 1.40 AM, taking twice as much time as necessary. Again what was it doing all this time? Did it air-drop arms for LTTE also? Or was it busy testing our surveillance and radar systems? Or checking on our nuclear plant at Kalapakkam and oil installations? The whole thing amounted to cocking a snook at India.

Interestingly enough the Purulia arms-dropping came to light only because a few hours earlier a five year young

girl, Priyanka, had been killed by a speeding bus and a thousand villagers were protesting her death, on the road. Otherwise this sinister incident would never have come to light!

When AN-26 was forced to land in Mumbai, it did not have to pay any airport fees, and it did not need any fuel. It had got fuel enough at Chennai to fly non-stop to Karachi. Why was Kim Davy, the chief villain of the piece, allowed to go to airport offices on the excuse of fuel and fees—and from there let to escape? According to West Bengal Government, Davy escaped from India via Nepal.

December 17 was a Sunday. Who at Varanasi airport got a bank manager to come on this holiday to open the bank and transact some financial business for Davy?

Is it a fact that we have permitted 45 air corridors? Why can't we have just a couple of them?

Is it also a fact that for more than two years before Purulia, we had no Director-General of Civil Aviation?

And is it a fact that neither in Varanasi, nor in Kolkata, nor in Chennai the plane's cargo and crew were checked?

At first the Government did suspend the Air Traffic Control officers in Chennai, Kolkata and Varanasi in view of the many lapses at different levels. But before long these suspension orders were withdrawn. Nobody likes to see any heads roll. But unless failures are identified and noted, how do we ensure compliance with standing orders in future? For, as Home Secretary K. Padmanabhan had candidly admitted to the Parliamentary Committee on Government Assurances, there was "total failure on the part of governmental agencies and there was total lack of coordination among them."

Perhaps the biggest single failure was in not taking due note of British Intelligence information on the subject passed on by RAW to Home. This information was passed

on to Bihar by fax. But it was sent to West Bengal only by a registered cover, which reached the State Chief Secretary only on December 26, nine days after the event. Union Joint Secretary Home Shashi Prakash's December 12 letter to N. Krishnamurthy, Chief Secretary, West Bengal, and the latter's January 4 letter to Union Home Secretary Shri Padmanabhan make reavealing reading.

Shashi Prakash's letter said:

"Dear Sir,

1. Reports available in this Ministry indicate that a Europe based businessman had approached an individual with a request to pilot a small plane between Karachi and Dhaka delivering arms and ammunition en route to communist rebels, in the area of Dhanbad. It was suggested to the pilot that he could land at an airstrip (86.20 degrees East and 24.30 degrees North) which is located along a river with hills on either side and close to the normal commercial air route from Karachi to Dhaka. After unloading the arms, the plane would go on to Dhaka, with its legitimate cargo.
2. The individual concerned is reported to have declined to take up the proposal. The arms dealer who was arranging the supply of the weapons is also learnt to have since pulled out of the deal on commercial grounds. Despite these setbacks, the businessman who approached the pilot has since purchased an AN-26 aircraft. He left for Riga, Latvia on November 15, 1995 and was planning to travel to Pakistan. Hence there is a strong possibility that he is still pursuing the project.
3. According to further information which, however, requires corroboration, the insurgent group which

was to receive 2,500 AK-47 weapons and 1,500,000 rounds of ammunition of Chinese make is opposed to CPM government in West Bengal. The plan was to air-lift the consignment of arms and ammunition to Karachi for storage by the side of the airport. From there the arms were to be placed on board a small aircraft, which would have filed a route to Dhaka but would make a brief unscheduled landing at a rough airstrip in an area called Panchat hill near Dhanbad.

4. Further enquiries reveal that there is a vast expanse of flat land near Panchat hill which is located about 5 km east of Nethuria police station, Purulia district, West Bengal. This used to be utilized as a fair weather airport some 20 years back by Calcutta companies having an interest in Dhanbad collieries. This location is about 9 km south of Panchat village and 8 km east of Chirkunda police station in Dhanbad district of Bihar. The place is sparsely populated but for about 400 Mahto tribals.
5. I shall be grateful if you could kindly sensitise the authorities concerned to be more vigilant and keep a close watch over the situation. We may also please be appraised of developments, if any in this regard."

***

And Shri Krishnamurthy's letter to Shri Padmanabhan said:

"I draw your kind attention to D.O. No. II-18015/3/95-ISD(A) dated 12th December, 1995 from the Joint Secretary, IS(I) addressed to me seeking to communicate the Intelligence relating to acquisition and dropping of arms and ammunition near Panchat hill about 5 km east of Nethuria police station in the district of Purulia.

"This communication was received here on 26th of December, 1995. The Registered Envelope shows the receipt at the Calcutta GPO on the 20th December, '95. I enclose a photocopy of this envelope for ready reference.

"As I had indicated to Shri V.K. Jain, the information which appears to have been available with the Army, Central Intelligence Agencies as also the Home Ministry was not shared with us at all in time. If the above mentioned communication had been dispatched through other available faster mechanism it would have been possible to take necessary precautionary measures. Unfortunately, the air-dropping took place on the night of 17th of December. In our view, it would have been possible to seize the entire consignment of arms and ammunition and we could also have possibly apprehended the recipients. We would also have had time to intercept the offending plane.

"I would request you to kindly have the matter looked into for appropriate steps."

***

However the British had also been less than straight with the Government of India. PTI reported from London: On March 7, "an adjournment motion was moved in the House of Commons alleging that British authorities had omitted significant portions from documents placed before the court of special judge hearing the sensational Purulia arms-drop case.

"The motion moved at the weekend by Tory MP from Southend at Sea in Essex, Sir Teddy Taylor, charged that the British government had deliberately 'altered and tampered' the vital piece of evidence of a hand-written note of a meeting between the main suspect, Peter Bleach and North Yorkshire police in September 1995.

"In the documents given to the Indian court, significant parts at the beginning and at the end have been removed,' the Tory MP, for whom arms-drop accused acted as a main constituency organizer, alleged in the Commons, while moving the adjournment motion on which the Home Secretary, Jack Straw would have to reply later this week.

"Claiming that he was not for 'any sort of interference with the Indian courts,' Taylor charged that the British government documents and evidence presented in the Indian court by Scotland Yard officer, Sergeant Elcock was, 'misrepresented evidence, with British police acting illegally to tamper with evidence presented before the court of special judge.'

"The arms-drop case, hearing for which is presently going on, is acquiring more and more mystery, with till date no mention having been made about who arranged and supplied the huge cache of lethal arms dropped at Purulia.

"Taylor claimed that in reply to his queries about Sergeant Elcock's deposition before the Calcutta court, he had been informed that there could have been 'clerical errors' by police in reproducing the documents of meeting with Bleach.

"He charged that Elcock had altered the document on instructions of MI-5, the main British internal security and intelligence agency. Taylor also claimed in the House that home department had not submitted the required P-II certificate to send these documents abroad.

"Taylor said as per his information and meetings with Peter Bleach in jail, Bleach had told him that he had recorded all telephonic talks with British special branch and MI-5 agents. 'But after police raids on Bleach's house and his disabled lady friend's house, all tapes except one are missing.'

"The Tory MP alleged that there was abundant evidence of official agencies trying to prevent courts in India knowing of close contacts between Bleach and British security agencies."

***

The Purulia conspiracy was hatched in a Hong Kong hotel in October 1985. Among those present were: Kim Davy, Joel Prorem and Joel's lawyer, Conrad Christian Bryan. They are all absconding. And all the lesser lights like Malhan brothers and Ansari brothers are out on bail. Many other shadowy figures flip through this drama. Davy's friends Satyanarayanan Gowda *alias* Randy and Daya Manikam Anand *alias* Dipak, were declared absconders. Kim's friend Martin Conrad Schneider uses six passports. They deal in arms, gold, drugs and uranium smuggling. It is a regular witches' cauldron. The CBI approached the CIA to verify the antecedents of Prorem, a US citizen, whose name surfaced while decoding different files in Kim Davy's lap-top computer, but CIA declined.

However, the characters which stand out prominently are the men who landed up in Mumbai. Five of them were Latvians from Russia who knew about Purulia but were not part of the conspiracy. They were hired as crew for some money ($ 7000). Although they had been sentenced for life they were let off on the urging of President Putin of Russia, on compassionate grounds, they being simple hirelings. But the two who stand out are Peter Bleach, Briton, and Kim Davy, the typical multinational, New Zealander-turned Dane.

Britain has been pressing India to let Peter Bleach go.

There have been over a dozen requests from their Prime Minister down. But his case stands on a different footing. He was the chief accomplice of Kim Davy in Operation Purulia. It was he who negotiated the purchase of AN-26 plane—equipped with portable global positioning for precision flying and landing—for $ 2,50,000, and got a cut of $ 25,000. Again it was he who obtained the fraudulent end-user certificate from the Bangladesh Government for the satisfaction of Bulgaria. And he was the man who was piloting the guilty plane. Britain cannot expect us to go soft on accused No. 2 unless they use their influence with the Danish or any other godfathers of Kim Davy, to extradite accused No.1, Davy, to India. And of that there is no hope.

Although the Danish Foreign Minister Prestig Moller had given hope to India's External Affairs Minister, last year, the Danish Prime Minister Anders Fogh Rasmussen did not respond to Vajpayeeji's assurance of justice tempered with mercy. Denmark even resented CBI visiting that country to investigate Davy. At the most, Denmark is willing to try Davy under its own law, which punishes illegal arms traders with just six months in jail. Meanwhile Kim Davy has became a media personality in Denmark. One Laila Miermont has even done the book *Weapons from Heaven* (Vaben Fra Himlen) on Davy's exploits. It is a mystery why Denmark is going out of its way to shield one of the eleven most Wanted Men in the world. In March 1997, Davy was even seen freely moving about in USA.

However the Question of Questions is: who commissioned Kim Davy to do a Purulia on India. VHP leader Ashok Singhal attributed it to "CIA *badmashi*". Veteran Muslim Leader Ali Mian of Lucknow also blamed CIA. In any case the Purulia Operation bore the multinational birthmarks of a CIA baby—with plane from Hong Kong, chief executive from a New Zealander-turned-

Dane, pilot from Britain, crew from Russia, arms from Bulgaria and parachutes from South Africa.

This impression was confirmed at a meeting of the Parliamentary Standing Committee on Defence held on March 7, 1996 in the Committee Room 'Main,' Parliament House Annexe. Apart from members of the Committee—and I was one of them from 1994-2000—the meeting was attended by Defence Secretary K.A. Nambiar, Home Secretary V.K. Jain, Civil Aviation Secretary Yogesh Chandra, CBI Director K. Vijaya Rama Rao, Air Marshal V.K. Bhatia, Air Vice-Marshal V.G. Kumar, Air Vice-Marshal Shahul, Commodore K.C. Phillipose, Director Operations (Air Defence) and their colleagues. Each one of them said that it was a CIA operation.

And when we adjourned for tea, one of them confided to me that since the plane had started from Pakistan, we all thought Pakistan had a hand in it. However fact was that CIA had launched this operation without taking even Pakistan's ISI (Inter-Services Intelligence) into confidence!

Such are the games USA's CIA plays. From Central Intelligence Agency, CIA has become Criminal Intelligence Agency.

Only a Comprehensive White Paper on Purulia can unravel the mystery of arms air-dropping which the Government aptly described as "waging war against India".